Praise for
YOUR SOUL IS THE SOURCE
OF YOUR POWER

'A clear and heartfelt guide to connecting with Spirit and discovering your true path.'
KYLE GRAY, SUNDAY TIMES BESTSELLING AUTHOR OF
ANGELS ARE WITH YOU NOW

'This is a beautifully written guide that reminds us: We're not here to find our spiritual power – it's already within us. As a medium and a teacher, Sean's ability to beautifully weave timeless spiritual truth and blend it with practical application is to be commended. This book will open your eyes to your divinity and empower you to live from the soul, embodying your own light and surrendering to the divine intelligence already within.'
JOHN HOLLAND, PSYCHIC MEDIUM, AUTHOR AND SPIRITUAL TEACHER

'Words such as sincere, honest, and kind easily come to mind when I think of Sean. Add to that accurate, compelling, and altogether talented in the field of mediumship and there he is! This book makes it clear that the spirit world are most invested in Sean's work and I know he'll go on to do marvellous things.'
TONY STOCKWELL, PSYCHIC MEDIUM, AUTHOR AND TEACHER

'Sean's book reminds us of the divine bridge between us and loved ones in spirit... revealing that energy doesn't die, and our hearts are not only physical, but resonant conductors and connectors of love.'
VEDA AUSTIN, WATER RESEARCHER, AUTHOR AND ARTIST

'*Your Soul is the Source of Your Power* is a beautifully written, deeply transformative guide to remembering your divine nature. Sean Collyns masterfully combines spiritual wisdom with practical insight, teaching readers to awaken their inner power and live in harmony with their higher selves.'

DANA-MAXX POMERANTZ, FOUNDER OF THE BE HAPPY PROJECT

YOUR SOUL IS THE SOURCE OF YOUR POWER

SEAN COLLYNS

HAY HOUSE

Carlsbad, California • New York City
London • Sydney • New Delhi

Published in the United Kingdom by:
Hay House UK Ltd, 1st Floor, Crawford Corner,
91–93 Baker Street, London W1U 6QQ
Tel: +44 (0)20 3927 7290; www.hayhouse.co.uk

Text © Sean Collyns, 2026
Interior images: Briarly Collyns and Shutterstock

The moral rights of the author have been asserted.

All rights reserved. No part of this book may be reproduced by any mechanical, photographic or electronic process, or in the form of a phonographic recording; nor may it be stored in a retrieval system, transmitted or otherwise be copied for public or private use, other than for 'fair use' as brief quotations embodied in articles and reviews, without prior written permission of the publisher.

The information given in this book should not be treated as a substitute for professional medical advice; always consult a medical practitioner. Any use of information in this book is at the reader's discretion and risk. Neither the author nor the publisher can be held responsible for any loss, claim or damage arising out of the use, or misuse, of the suggestions made, the failure to take medical advice or for any material on third-party websites.

A catalogue record for this book is available from the British Library.

Tradepaper ISBN: 978-1-83782-472-4
E-book ISBN: 978-1-83782-475-5
Audiobook ISBN: 978-1-83782-473-1

10 9 8 7 6 5 4 3 2 1

This product uses responsibly sourced papers, including recycled materials and materials from other controlled sources. For more information, see www.hayhouse.co.uk

The authorized representative in the EU for product safety and compliance is Penguin Random House Ireland, Morrison Chambers, 32 Nassau Street, Dublin D02 YH68, Ireland. https://eu-contact.penguin.ie

Printed and bound by CPI Group (UK) Ltd, Croydon CR0 4YY

*You are divinity incarnate, miracles
encapsulated, and power infinite.*

*Welcome to your remembrance, friend.
This book is dedicated to you.*

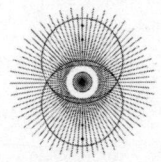

CONTENTS

Foreword by Anita Moorjani ... ix
Invocation ... xv
Introduction ... xvii

PART I: SOUL

Chapter 1: Forgetting, to Remember ... 5
Chapter 2: The Soul's Greatest Battle: The Ego ... 27
Chapter 3: The Soul's Journey to Earth ... 43

PART II: SOURCE

Chapter 4: Your True Home ... 63
Chapter 5: Why You Left Home ... 75
Chapter 6: Soul Friends: Guides, Guardians, Helpers ... 91

PART III: POWER

Chapter 7: Tending the Soul's Gateway ... 113
Chapter 8: Harnessing Your Soul's Power ... 123

Chapter 9:	Learning Your Own Language	143
Chapter 10:	Illuminating the Darkness	153
Chapter 11:	Discovering Your Infinite Potential	169
Chapter 12:	The Alchemy of Belief: How Miracles Become Reality	177
Chapter 13:	Spirit-Led Manifesting: Weaving Your Soul's Destiny	193
Chapter 14:	Mediumship: Communicating with the Spirit World	211
Chapter 15:	Returning to Connection	233

Conclusion: The Guiding Light to Purpose	243
Closing Invocation	249
Final Note	251
Further Reading	253
Acknowledgments	254
About the Author	257

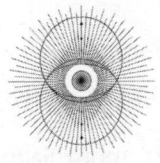

FOREWORD

There are rare moments in life when we encounter souls who seem to bridge the gap between the seen and the unseen, the known and the unknowable – people whose presence alone carries the resonance of something beyond this world. Meeting Sean Collyns was one of those moments for me.

As someone who has walked the delicate line between life and death, who has touched the vast, limitless love of the other side and returned with an awakened understanding, I have learned to recognize those who carry the same depth of knowing. Sean is one of those luminous beings – someone who moves between worlds with grace, wisdom, and an open heart.

When I was asked to write this foreword for Sean's book, I didn't hesitate for a moment. Over the years, I have met many extraordinary spiritual teachers, healers, and mediums, each bringing their own unique light to the world. But there is something about Sean that stands apart. He doesn't just communicate with the spirit realm, he embodies its messages, weaving them into profound yet practical guidance for those of us navigating the human experience.

What touches me most about Sean's work is his integrity. In a field that is often met with skepticism or clouded by misconception, he stands unwavering in truth and humility. He does not seek to dazzle with spectacle or claim grandiosity – his gift is not about performance, but about service. With deep sincerity, he offers himself as a bridge, bringing comfort, healing, and a greater understanding of the infinite nature of our existence. He approaches his work not with ego, but with a genuine desire to help others feel less alone, more connected, and profoundly loved.

Sean's journey has not been without its challenges, as is often the case for those called to this path. From a young age, he was aware of his extraordinary abilities, yet like many of us who are drawn to the mystical, he had to navigate doubt, fear, and the weight of understanding a reality that others could not always see. It was through these experiences – through the struggles and the revelations – that he honed his gifts, emerging as the compassionate, courageous medium he is today.

This book is more than just an exploration of the spirit world – it is an invitation to remember who we truly are. Through Sean's words, we are reminded that death is not an ending, but a continuation. That love does not vanish when a physical body ceases to be. That our departed loved ones remain with us, revealing their presence in quiet moments, guiding us, comforting us, and reminding us that we are never truly alone.

One of the most beautiful aspects of Sean's work is his unwavering focus on love as the ultimate force of healing. On my own journey, I have come to understand that love is not simply an emotion, it is the very fabric of our being. It is what binds us together, beyond time, beyond space, beyond lifetimes. Sean's messages from Spirit return again and again to the truth that love never dies. It transforms, it expands, it reaches across dimensions, holding us in ways we may not always see, but can always feel.

This book is filled with stories that will stir your soul and open your heart. Whether you're grieving a loss, searching for answers, or simply curious about what lies beyond the veil, you will find solace in these pages.

Sean speaks with such clarity, warmth, and tenderness that his words feel less like reading and more like remembering – remembering that there is more to this life than meets the eye, that we are held in the embrace of something vast and beautiful, and that we are always, always loved.

As I read through Sean's words, I was reminded of something profound yet simple: the importance of living fully, here and now. So often, we become lost in the distractions of daily life, forgetting the deeper truths that pulse beneath the surface. Sean's work is a gentle but powerful call to awaken – to slow down, to listen, to trust that we are guided by forces greater than ourselves. The spirit world is not some distant place, it is intertwined with our existence, woven into our every breath, our every moment.

Sean's devotion to his calling is an inspiration. He doesn't just share messages from beyond, he teaches us how to open our own hearts to the whispers of Spirit, to recognize the signs, to trust the love that continues even after physical separation. His work is a lighthouse for those who feel lost, a reminder that even in the darkest of times, we are never without guidance, never without love.

On my own journey, I have often spoken about the courage it takes to embrace the unknown, to walk through life with open hands and an open heart. This book is an invitation to do just that – to explore, to wonder, to trust. It reminds us that life is not merely what we can see, touch, and measure – it is infinite, unfolding, and filled with unseen miracles. Our loved ones who have crossed over are not gone; they are closer than we think, loving us, supporting us, guiding us in ways we are only beginning to understand.

As you turn these pages, I encourage you to read not just with your mind, but with your heart. Let these stories awaken something within you. Let them bring comfort, understanding, and maybe even a little bit of magic into your life. Whether you're seeking peace, clarity, or simply a sense of connection, know that you're exactly where you're meant to be – and that love, in all its endless forms, is right there with you.

Sean Collyns is more than a medium – he is a teacher, a healer, a messenger of hope. His work is a testament to the truth that we are all interconnected, not just to one another, but to the universe itself. The spirit world is not separate from our own, but a continuation of it, woven into the very essence of who we are. Sean's ability to bring forth its messages of love, healing, and hope is a gift to us all, and I am honored to write this foreword as he shares his gift with the world.

As you begin this journey through Sean's book, may you feel the presence of those who love you, both in this world and beyond. May you find peace in knowing that life never truly ends, it simply transforms. And may you remember, always, that you are deeply, infinitely loved.

Much Love,
Anita
Anita Moorjani, *New York Times* best-selling author

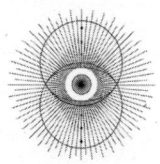

INVOCATION

Hi there, Divine Being,

I see you've found yourself here on Planet Earth, doing the 'human thing' again. I know sometimes it feels like you must have skipped the fine print before arriving, and now you're wondering what the hell you're doing here. But let me assure you, you knew exactly what you were getting yourself into.

One of the conditions of this journey was amnesia. You agreed to forget who you were so that you could rediscover yourself, piece by piece, through experience. In ultimate truth, you are an eternal spark of divine consciousness. The you who is reading these words right now is just one expression, one facet, one moment in the vastness of your existence.

Amid the noise and weight of this world, remembering that truth isn't always easy. And yet, here you are. Just by picking up this book, you've already answered the call of your soul – a call to remember.

Let this be a journey of remembrance. As you move through these pages, you will begin to feel something stir within you – an ancient knowing, a resonance that reminds you of what has always been. Through the wisdom and techniques shared here, your connection to the spirit within and around you will awaken, and new abilities will come online. Your soul is powerful beyond measure. It always has been. This is simply your time to remember.

So, take a deep breath.

Open your heart.

Let's begin.

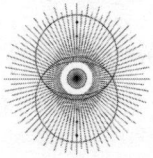

INTRODUCTION

Many people look at the world around them and see all that exists as some kind of miraculous accident or fluke. They believe that the planet we inhabit was once just microscopic grains of stardust drifting through space and transformed into a beautiful oasis for millions of different life-forms to exist and thrive upon, all by sheer coincidence. To them, there is no unseen intelligent force orchestrating it all. There is no magic within how our very existence has come about.

The perspective of those many individuals demonstrates the condition that we enter this world with: amnesia.

They are yet to discover that there is a universe of infinite power and potential lying dormant within them, a power they are made up of – and ironically are yet to believe in.

That amnesia can be one of the toughest conditions to break out of. You may be reading this right now, wholeheartedly considering yourself 'a believer,' yet still in this trap because you're yet to truly believe that the power I speak of is actually within your reach. It can be nearly impossible to perceive yourself as a unique spark of the divine intelligent force that orchestrates the entire universe – but that is exactly what you are.

And that is exactly what I'm here to help you remember.

I am a medium. I communicate with the spirit world, deliver messages from those who are there, and teach their philosophies and wisdom. It is the greatest honor to be their ambassador. To have the opportunity to be a conduit of the ongoing love that exists between their world and ours.

Ours is a skeptical world, so I've spent a lot of my time demonstrating that the spirit world exists. Giving proof that our loved ones in spirit are in fact still with us, watching over us, guiding us.

But this book isn't here to convince anyone that the spirit world exists. It isn't for those yet to be convinced that there's more to this world than meets the eye. It's for those who have already started to remember. Those who have seen or sensed the magic that is possible in this world and felt it stir something within them. A familiarity. A knowing. A sense of something much greater. A resonant understanding that death isn't the end, just as birth wasn't the beginning.

So, the point of this book isn't to open rigid minds. It is to help those who are ready to access their soul's power and fulfil the divine potential that resides within them. To live a life that is connected to their spirit, and led by it.

And it begins with you – with the light at your core that is as ancient as time itself. The light that has all the secrets of this universe encoded within it. The light that is miracles and magic encapsulated. The light that is eternal, everlasting, and ever-expanding. The light that you are.

And that light is part of something even greater – an intelligence beyond comprehension, a light that is consciousness itself. Whether you want to call it Source, Grand Spirit, God, or the Universe (and feel free throughout this book to use whichever term best aligns with you), it is the consciousness that you were born from. It is what you are made up of. It is what you will always be.

And whether you know it or not, you have found yourself here because you're seeking a deeper connection with that truth, and with that light. You're here to embody your divine power and unlock deeper levels of your potential in this life. And trust me when I say it is grander than you could have ever believed.

You didn't end up here in the midst of all the beautiful chaos of this world by accident. You made a conscious and purposeful decision to come here. And not only that – you chose every aspect of it. Down to the last detail, like the exact minute and location you would enter. You decided where the cosmos would be placed around you at that exact moment, so that the magnetic force of the planets and stars would influence your personality, traits, and even your downfalls, in specific ways. Just as the moon pulls upon the ocean and its tides, you decided how the cosmos would pull upon your own emotional world and its ebbs and flows.

I know what you're thinking: *I must have chosen wrong!*

But let me reassure you, you didn't.

Your life may not be a joyride, but you didn't come here for that. Your journey is far more purposeful.

You came here to be immersed within the magic, the wonder, and also the pain and the loss that were waiting to be experienced here. Every hurdle, every conflict, every heartbreak or 'dark night of the soul' that you face is seen by your soul as an opportunity to grow and learn something new. Your soul chose the exact curriculum it wanted to be faced with in coming here to 'Earth School.'

However, it didn't get to choose how you would navigate that curriculum. That's on you.

Many wonder why a soul – a ball of conscious intelligent light, vibrating with the frequencies of euphoric love, expansive joy, and miracles – would ever choose an earthly existence. But imagine if that intelligence just drifted through the cosmos for eternity...

I once asked the spirit world to show me what it was like to exist in our original and pure state, and what made a soul wish to come here. They told me, 'It's like constantly being filled with the feeling that you want to get up and dance, but never having a body to do it with.'

> **Your soul came here to dance, to create, to expand, and to evolve.**

It came here for the moments – moments of amazement and wonder, moments of laughter and joy, moments of love and connection, moments of compassion, growth, and learning.

Introduction

To your soul, a life filled with beautiful moments is a life of true wealth, meaning, and value. That seems so obvious, yet is so easily forgotten in the madness of our world.

This book is a portal to those moments. It's a guide to soul embodiment, to strengthening spiritual connection and unlocking spiritual abilities, to living the most soulful and purposeful of existences, overflowing with abundance of the truest kind and illuminated by the most divine light – the light of your true self.

Wherever you find yourself picking up this book right now, even if you've never had a spiritual experience before, even if you think you lack 'natural ability,' this exploration will trigger an awakening within you. I am truly excited for you.

✦ ✦ ✦

As someone who rediscovered their spiritual abilities and connection to the spirit world at the age of 15, I have spent my entire adulthood thus far (and most of my teens) dedicated to uncovering the mysteries of the spiritual realms and the way we are able to access them. This has been a pathway that has been as confronting and demanding as it has been awe-inspiring and magical in all imaginable ways.

Through my unfoldment as a medium, I have uncovered the secrets used for centuries to perform the miracle of mediumship – to speak with the spirit world in vivid detail and with profound energy. What I have discovered is that the energy mediums harness to connect with Spirit lives within every soul. And it's available to anyone.

It's a power that doesn't just have the potential to open the gate to the other world, but to transform the one you're living in, too. It can guide you into a life infused with magic. Where beautiful manifestations flow into your world with ease. Where miracles are natural and frequent. Where your divine intelligence leads the way, and your soul's desires align with the very pathway you find yourself on. Where your perception of what is possible for yourself is completely transformed.

I'll never forget my own overwhelming excitement every time I unlocked a new ability. The first time I communicated with a spirit and was able to receive undeniable validation of my experience was with my sister's spirit guide. She appeared to me vividly – I remember seeing her deeply colored robes, large bangles, and decorative headpiece – and everything in her essence exuded royal energy. I felt sure she was a princess of some kind. While connecting to her, I saw camels walking through the desert with cargo on their backs and I felt a strong connection to somewhere in the Middle East. She told me her name was Emily, a name I doubted after my impression of an Arabian location – Emily Ru.

'Ru-something,' I said to my sister. 'She's also telling me that we will find her, that her story is known.'

I didn't know where this was all coming from, I just felt so deeply that it was true. We excitedly went straight to Google, and I believe the search we did was: '*Emily Ru. Arabia. Princess*.'

And there she was – on the front cover of a book, *Memoirs of an Arabian Princess from Zanzibar* by Emily Ruete. She was dressed in the beautiful robes, the bangles, and the headpiece that I had seen.

That moment changed everything for me.

Then there was the first time I manifested something against all the odds – an experience that cemented my understanding of the power of intentional creation and alignment. At 16, I had tickets to see my all-time favorite artist, the Princess of Pop herself: Kylie Minogue. I had adored her since before I could speak. (In fact, 'Kylie Minogue' may well have been my very first spoken words.) Now I had a wild thought: *What if I could get up on stage and meet her?* It was the perfect opportunity to put every manifestation technique I had been learning about to the test.

In the days leading up to the concert, I became absolutely certain within every cell of my being that she was going to call me up on stage. I told all of my colleagues at the café where I worked that I was going to see Kylie that weekend and that she was going to call me up on stage with her. They laughed, wishing me luck.

The day of the concert I had a last-minute thought. Something told me go to the store, buy a large piece of paper and write her a message. The show was part of her 'Kiss Me Once' tour, so I wrote: 'Kylie, will you kiss me once?'

The night of the concert, as I stood in line, I felt sick to my stomach. I believed so wholeheartedly that it was about to happen that I went green in the face from nerves.

I just knew it was coming, and it was. Just after she'd hit the high notes of 'Your Disco Needs You,' a member of her team handed her a water bottle to take a drink from. In perfect sync with her turning her head from the audience to take a sip, a cameraman turned his camera on me, and my image – and my sign – came up on a large monitor, right in Kylie's line of sight.

She read out the message, and began singing a song directly to me while gesturing me to come up on stage. Then there I was, in a complete fluster, standing in front of 13,000 people, face to face with Kylie. She planted a kiss on my cheek and I grabbed a selfie to treasure the moment.

The next day, the local newspaper ran the headline: 'Teen Sean Collyns left spinning around after being kissed by Kylie Minogue.' I couldn't wait to show it to my work colleagues.

It was a manifestation so seamless, so undeniable, that I knew there was an incredible power at play within me, one stronger than I had ever known, a power that was capable of aligning me with my wildest dreams.

Then came the first time I consciously induced an out-of-body experience (OBE), otherwise known as astral projection. This is the experience of separating your consciousness from your physical body and venturing through inter-dimensional spaces. For weeks, I had practiced this particular technique as it was suggested and, although I was feeling profound sensations, I was yet to succeed in getting 'out of my body.' Then one afternoon, as I sat on my balcony, I noticed the sunlight refracting through the glass, forming a beautiful rainbow-colored 'X' on the floor. Something told me to lie within those beams of light.

Introduction

With the rainbow X landing perfectly across my chest, I felt the most powerful energy beginning to activate within me. I began the technique once more, feeling my astral body detaching from my physical body... and suddenly a portal opened at the center of my vision, its edges made up of the same rainbow-colored light that was crossing my chest. And there I was, standing, looking down at my own body lying on the floor.

I heard the front door to the apartment open, and immediately I was there in front of it. My roommate came inside and passed straight through me like a scene in some ghost movie. I saw her put her things down and immediately pick up the hairbrush that was on her nightstand and almost compulsively begin to brush her hair. Later when I asked her if this was what had happened, she said that her hair had been bothering her all afternoon and she couldn't wait to get home to brush it. She had no idea how I could possibly have known that, and I decided not to divulge the details.

But I hadn't spent all that time practicing so that I could spy on my roommate! It was time to explore.

I moved back out to where my body was lying and thought about flying. As soon as I thought about it, it was happening. I was hovering outside my apartment, looking back at it from five stories above street level.

Up there, I thought about all the places I could visit, and as I did so, I shot up into the sky at lightning speed. I found myself looking down on the Earth, and from this unbound moment, as soon as I thought of a place I would like to go, I'd find myself coming down toward it from above.

After much exploring, the final destination I arrived at was my grandmother's house in New Zealand. The roof was unmistakable from above. Then I found myself standing in her living room. It was that time of the evening when she would sit with a glass of wine and watch her favorite shows, which was exactly how I saw her.

What I was blown away to see was my grandfather standing beside her. He had passed away many years prior to this time. The way I saw him was the same way I was seeing myself – we were translucent. I could see my gran and her living room as though I was actually there, but while I could see my grandfather's face and his outline, I could see straight through him too. He was in an astral form, just as I was. His spirit was able to meet me in that place *in between* and give me a very important message.

He looked me in the eye and said, 'Sean, you are a medium. How many signs do we need to send you for you to begin trusting yourself? There is a man named Tony Stockwell coming to Melbourne this March. He has mastered the art of mediumship – he can help you. Go and learn from him.'

Upon returning to my body, the first thing I did was go straight to my phone to search the information while it was fresh in my mind. And there it was: 'Tony Stockwell Mediumship Seminar' starting on 27 March.

Within a month, I was there and my formal training had begun. I expanded majorly within that week. For the first time I found a sense of trust and confidence in my spiritual connection, and it propelled me toward offering my services

Introduction

to the public and stepping onto the pathway I have been on since then.

✦ ✦ ✦

The purpose of sharing all of these experiences isn't to make you think that I'm special, but to show you the kind of things you're capable of too. I don't believe there is such a thing as a 'gifted' person – there are only those who have been able to *remember* enough to access the power of their soul and those who are yet to remember.

Abilities like spirit communication, manifestation, astral projection, clairvoyance, telepathy, remote viewing, energy healing, and even telekinesis and weather manipulation are all within your potential. Learning to access those superpowers within you is a process of understanding and removing the layers and walls that are keeping you at a distance from what is at your core – infinite power.

On my own journey, I have come up against many of those barriers, and throughout this book I will share the understandings and approaches that have helped me (and continue to help me) move beyond them.

Each chapter of this book is designed to take you deeper into your soul's power. We'll explore the nature of your soul, and the place from which it originates. You'll find guided exercises and practical steps designed to bring you closer to your most soul-embodied self.

This book is a guide to becoming magical AF. With willingness, excitement, and a little patience, you will find it leading you to experiences that will change your perception of yourself – and the reality that you experience – forever.

If you can promise to stick with me and implement the understandings, perspectives, and techniques we'll cover together here, I can promise you a completely reborn version of yourself.

Your soul brought you here. And the nature of your soul is where we begin.

Part I
SOUL

Your soul is the source of your power, and it's a unique spark of the most divine intelligence.

This book is a guide back to your soul.

It's not just here to inspire you, it's here to activate you.

Within these pages, you'll uncover a deeper understanding of your existence and remember what your soul has always known: that you are powerful, connected, and capable of extraordinary things.

This isn't about becoming something new. It's about returning to the truth of who and what you already are.

Let this be your invitation to step into who you are – and let your soul lead the way.

The nature of your soul is where we begin. You have a world of power within you, waiting to be remembered.

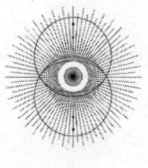

Chapter 1

FORGETTING, TO REMEMBER

I was very lucky to grow up in a family that was open to the spirit world, mediums, and psychics. Esoteric concepts were spoken about openly. A core childhood memory of mine is of my father tying one of my grandfather's old suit cufflinks to a piece of string and using it to communicate with his spirit by asking 'yes' or 'no' questions as you would with a pendulum. It responded, and we all felt his spirit was there with us.

I think it runs in our blood to be this way – we even had a distant relative who was publishing books about UFOs back in the 1970s. So, you could say I was blessed from the beginning to have an openness to such topics. Or doomed – whichever way you wish to see it!

That openness in my family is what allowed me to begin exploring my abilities and potential at a younger age than most people get the chance to. I remember being sent to bed but, knowing my parents were just down the hallway watching *Crossing Over with John Edward*, not being able to resist sneaking out and trying to catch a glimpse of it.

I remember sitting in amazement behind the wall, with one eye peering around the corner, watching over my parents' shoulders, trying not to make a sound. I'd stay there as long as I could without getting busted – which, of course, I always was.

I was completely infatuated. I believed that to receive such detailed information about people who'd passed away, John Edward must have been experiencing it all really viscerally. I imagined it was like having someone speaking directly into his ear, or standing in front of him, giving him messages. Or maybe it was like a movie screen being projected into his mind, spelling out words or replaying the memories of those who had transitioned. I just couldn't comprehend how else it could be possible to bring such detailed stories to life.

I remember feeling so lit up watching him, thinking, *Wow, if only I could do that one day.* But I saw his abilities as a gift and felt that he was doing something that very few others were capable of. Since I'd never experienced what I assumed he was experiencing, I thought I hadn't been given that gift and didn't have the potential to do what he was doing, even though while watching him, there was a spark igniting inside me that was telling me the opposite.

It took me a long time to break out of that perspective. Even after having many of my own experiences and encounters with Spirit, I still saw mediums as different from everyone else.

My father was very psychic and open to the spirit world himself. He had a natural receptivity that I'm sure I picked up from him. My grandmother, his mum, was the same. Dad would randomly, and on a whim, predict celebrity deaths.

He predicted Elvis's, Charlie Chaplin's, and other well-known individuals' unexpected passings with very precise timing. He had many spiritual experiences and encounters, but as a business-oriented, structural-thinking man, he never explored it deeply. He'd always joke, 'Well, what use would I be just predicting famous people's deaths?'

Even with his openness and clear ability, I still didn't think either of us was capable of doing what someone like John Edward could do.

Then, at 15, I had my first reading. It was with an incredible medium named Debbie Mewes. I had no idea what to expect, say, or do. All I knew was my mum had been to see this woman and had decided every one of us needed to go too. As soon as possible.

This will give you an idea of how clueless I was. I was to bring a personal object along for the medium to hold on to, something that would assist her in connecting to my energy. I had no idea what to take – I got myself into a fluster trying to think of the perfect thing – and what I ended up deciding on was... my collection of baby teeth.

I'm still mortified to this day that I handed her a little tub of my old teeth. But we laugh about it now.

Regardless, she was a professional, and she got on with the session. She blew me away with her connection – it was undeniable. She knew things that I hadn't told anyone.

Although her accuracy was astounding, there was one thing she said to me that I was absolutely certain she was wrong about.

She looked me in the eye and said, 'I know you are young to be told this... but you are a medium.'

That's when I thought to myself, *Maybe she's not as good as I thought she was.*

Then she went on to say, 'I don't just feel that you have a natural connection and potential, but I feel you have very big potential and you will be very well known for this one day.'

Me? A medium? The idea was ridiculous to me. I had never seen an apparition or made any kind of psychic prediction, so how could I ever possibly develop the skills that she had?

Then she went on to compare the potential that she felt within me to none other than John Edward.

And as my mind was scoffing at the nonsensical words coming from her mouth, something was happening in my body: Everything within me was lighting up with a fluttery feeling that was deeper than hope. It was the feeling I remembered having as a child while hiding behind the wall watching John Edward, but far bigger. It was a knowingness.

'Yes!' my soul was screaming, but my mind was clearly not ready to accept it.

Despite my doubts and the feeling that I knew better, there *was* a little part of me that wondered if maybe, just maybe, she wasn't *entirely* wrong. She had just demonstrated that she could interpret energy very well, after all.

As it turned out, it seemed she *was* onto something...

Moving Beyond Expectation

That day sparked something within me. I began learning. I spent my weekend-job paycheck on my first deck of tarot cards. My first pendulum. Started a crystal collection. You know – the usual woo-woo awakening starter pack.

Some out-of-the-ordinary occurrences started happening too. I began seeing, sensing, and feeling things from time to time. I would see things that 'weren't there' in old places. I was having encounters with spirits. But there was a part of me that believed I was just making it all up. Or that perhaps it *was* happening, but it wasn't strong or profound enough to make me a medium. It wouldn't be until years later that the spirit world started showing up for me in a way that made me realize I *could* actually be that.

I'll tell you about that soon. But what's important for you to know right now, and the reason I'm sharing all of this, is because almost everyone has the same barrier in their mind as I did.

And that barrier is *expectation*.

Through developing my mediumship abilities and offering readings, I discovered that my initial assumptions about the way mediumship worked were actually shared by many. Most people I came across looked at the work I was doing and the connection I had with Spirit the same way I once viewed John Edward's connection – as some rare ability gifted to a select few. And they thought that for mediums to receive clear, detailed messages from spirit, they must be seeing and hearing them in a similar way to how we see with our eyes and hear with our ears.

But it isn't like that.

And the biggest thing that stops the majority of people from connecting with the spirit world themselves is the expectation of how clear that interaction should be.

When people begin trying to access their spiritual abilities, they unconsciously chase a certain kind of experience – something loud, dramatic, or impossible to miss. That expectation is what blocks them from sensing what's already there. If you take one thing from this chapter, let it be this:

You must release the need for certainty and develop trust in the subtle.

And hear me when I say this: the ability to communicate with Spirit isn't something you inherit or are specially selected for. The ability to perceive energy, be psychic, or be a powerful manifestor or energy healer is never something that people are gifted with. These are things that your soul has always inherently known and been capable of.

You've simply *forgotten*. And this journey is about remembering.

Remembering Who You Really Are

The majority of people go all the way through life without being certain of what they're capable of, or even whether there is an afterlife. There are, however, a small number who get to proceed through this world entirely and undoubtedly *knowing* that there is more to come, and some have reawakened psychic abilities as well. All of them have been in a situation that would have been considered extremely unlucky at the time: they've died and been brought back to life.

It's a wondrous thing to explore the experiences of these people. In doing so, it's impossible to deny the common threads and similarities between their individual near-death experiences (NDEs). This is what's most often described:

- a euphoric sense of relief from any physical pain, fear, or sadness

- a brilliant warm and embracing light that they are enveloped by

- being met by an angelic-like guardian figure or a loved one

- a moment in time where they're shown their entire life all at once, they remember every decision and action they ever took, and they sense the ripple effects of each of those actions from an expanded awareness

- a deep sense of being 'home' in a state of complete bliss, embraced by divine love

- (and often) a desire to stay exactly where they are, rather than return to their physical body, yet a feeling that they must return.

This vivid encounter easily establishes a deep sense of trust within the experiencer of their true eternal nature. It changes their entire perspective of themselves from that point onward, and therefore the way that they experience themselves.

Experiencers often report 'coming back' with stronger psychic abilities and enhanced intuition, as well as more frequent and vivid interactions with the spirit world – almost as though in momentarily *going* to the spirit world, they have brought a piece of it back with them. What this experience really does for people is cure the amnesia that they came into this world with.

Have you ever met a person who 'almost died' and then started seeing spirits? It's a real phenomenon. Many renowned and respected mediums, including some of my colleagues, first became aware of their ability to communicate with Spirit through an NDE.

Upon further investigation of these cases, it becomes clear that not only is the spiritual connection activated in a way that makes psychic phenomena become more prominent occurrences for these individuals, but physical phenomena in their environment are frequently reported too.

A study published by the University of Virginia found that people who'd been through a near-death experience were three times more likely to experience 'electromagnetic phenomena' than someone who had not.[1]

---

1. Greyson, B., *et al.* (2015), 'Electromagnetic Phenomena Reported by Near-Death Experiencers,' *Journal of Near-Death Studies*, 33(4), Summer.

The phenomena reported were things like lights flickering, clocks stopping and starting, interference around technology and radios, etc.

Seemingly, these people *came back* from the near-death experience awakened, activated, and more deeply connected in all ways.

The difference between a person who's had an NDE and a person who hasn't, is that the person who's had an NDE has been reminded, through a vivid first-hand experience, of their divine and eternal nature.

The human experience is one where we're tricked into believing that who we are right now is the be-all and end-all – a perspective that limits our innate connection to our own divinity. The advantage these experiencers have is that their NDE has reminded them that they are much more, and with this realization, they cannot help but become a greater embodiment of their soul, and progress through their life in an entirely different way because of it.

> *'You can't die for the life of you.'*
> DORIS STOKES

People who have had an NDE are often awakened not only to their own power and potential, but also to a deeper sense of purpose in their life.

Although it may seem that these people have somehow 'brought back' a piece of the spirit world with them from their visit, the only thing they truly bring back from that experience is the *memory* of it.

Through their experiences, we're able to gain vital understandings. It becomes abundantly clear that the secret to accessing our soul power lies within the lens through which we perceive ourselves. If you perceive yourself to be a human being in the most basic sense, through physicality alone, you will experience yourself as just that and nothing more. However, if you perceive yourself to be an eternal spark of divinity and power that is temporarily inhabiting a human existence, then you'll begin to experience your divine nature and capabilities more and more.

To shift your lens of perception is to completely reframe your belief system. Aside from those rare circumstances, it takes discipline, mindful awareness, and repetitive action.

We often believe that only that which we can experience with our most basic of human senses is real. That's why the undeniable, vivid experience of an NDE has the potential to change beliefs and transform a person's life with almost immediate effect.

But don't worry, coming close to death isn't the *only* pathway to spiritual empowerment. To rewire your beliefs and transform the way you're experiencing yourself, *you just have to find ways to remember who and what you truly are.*

While some people might naturally gravitate toward or have a knack for certain abilities, none of it is exclusive. You don't need to be accepted into some kind of spiritual elite to experience your own soul's power.

I always say mediumship is like singing. Everyone can do it. Some are naturals. Many can learn to hold a note. Some are the next Whitney Houston. Others should maybe keep it to the privacy of their own homes. But everyone *can* sing. And everyone can enjoy singing.

The same goes for *all* spiritual abilities. They aren't things you need to earn or become worthy of. They are doorways. And the key to unlocking those doorways is trust.

You open them by tuning into the slightest shifts in your awareness. The nuanced energies emerging within and around you.

Because it's all energy.

Before you became physical, you were energy too. Energy is your soul's first language. It's your most innate form of communication.

That's why soul-to-soul communication isn't just something 'mediums' do – it's the original language of the soul. It's how we communicated before we came here, and how we'll communicate when we return home to spirit.

The 'ability' is simply the remembrance of that language and the quietening of all the noise that made you forget.

So if you've been called to this book to explore your spiritual connection, your power, or your intuitive gifts, whether for mediumship, healing, guidance, or manifestation, just know:

What you're accessing isn't new. It isn't outside of you. It's something you've carried within your soul since the very beginning.

You're not learning it, you're remembering it.

And chances are... you've already experienced it.

The Switches We Turned Off

Have you ever wondered why some children seem to be able to recall past lives, describe family members they never had the chance to meet, or speak of events they couldn't possibly know about? Many have imaginary friends, ones who seem a little too real at times... Or have you heard of those rare cases of xenoglossy, the phenomenon of children being fluent in a language that they've had absolutely no exposure to? Not in their current lifetime anyway...

Children are among the most spiritually connected of us all – and for good reason. But there's also a reason why these abilities fade, why their unseen playmates disappear, and why those eerie, seemingly unexplainable memories seem to vanish as they grow older.

Early Disconnections

As we grow up, our minds are shaped by our environment, our upbringing, and everything we are exposed to or sheltered from. During that time, our sense of 'what we know' – or more accurately, 'what we think we know' – becomes further defined. Through increasing cognition, belief systems about reality take root within us, formed through pathways in our brains. These ingrained beliefs then dictate how we perceive and experience life, limiting us within a framework of our own creation. Our minds become programmed to filter information in a way that subconsciously seems most useful to us. And unfortunately, due to the mind's tendency to attach to the material, we often condition ourselves to disconnect from anything that extends beyond it.

Understanding how your mind was programmed in early childhood is one of the keys to unlocking your dormant spiritual abilities, since that is when they were first suppressed. The process of discovering and harnessing your spiritual abilities can often be like finding switches you never knew you turned off and learning how to turn them back on.

Seeing What's Important

Your brain has an amazing way of only showing you the things that it's been led to understand as 'important.' A perfect example of this is how it removes your nose from your vision. Have you ever noticed that your nose isn't constantly in the way of whatever you're looking at throughout your day, and it isn't until you think about seeing your nose that you realize it's been within your visual field the entire time?

Your clever little brain has done you the favor of getting it out of your way, so that you can enjoy unobstructed vision. And now that I've said it, it's all that you can see... Sorry about that.

In a similar way, in our upbringings, most of us are conditioned to believe that only what we can experience with our most basic senses is real. Unconsciously, we disregard everything else as 'unimportant information,' discrediting our extra-sensory perception and shutting down the part of ourselves that connects to the unseen and intangible. So we disconnect from the subtle energetic realms surrounding us, because they aren't part of the 'reality' we're taught about.

Therefore, in order to proceed further into our own soul's greatness, we must reflect upon the earliest decisions we made about the nature of this reality and reintroduce optimistic perspectives that are aligned with infinite possibility.

You could compare the way your brain functions to a spotlight in a dark theatre. It focuses only on what it has been told is important, and everything else remains unnoticed, in the dark. All of these miraculous abilities of your soul, like clairvoyance and spirit communication, are just things that have been disregarded by your brain as unimportant. They aren't missing, they're just dormant. They've been left standing in the wings, and they're waiting for their cue.

The Great Loss of Imagination

Do you remember a time when your dreams felt so incredibly real that on waking in the morning, you believed they were a genuine experience? Or a time when your nightmares were so vivid that you actually believed you were really seeing monsters and dark, scary things lurking in your room at night-time?

As a child, those things feel so real that they become difficult to distinguish from your waking reality. Also, we aren't really taught how to differentiate between authentic spiritual experiences and our highly active imagination.

I remember having a dream once that I was flying. In it, I awoke, lying with my back against the ceiling, looking down at my body in bed. I floated through the house, out of the front door, and up into the night sky, soaring through space looking down on the Earth below. It was magical.

I now understand that this experience was my first memorable out-of-body experience. But at the time, I believed so wholeheartedly that what I'd 'dreamed' was real that the next day I attempted to jump off my bed and fly again. The reality check of falling flat on my face made me feel silly. I decided I'd just made the whole thing up. But I hadn't. That experience had been real. And it had been different from my other dreams for a reason.

Situations like this are where our perception of realms beyond the material often gets dismissed as 'just imagination.' Because of that harsh reality check I disregarded what had actually been a profound spiritual experience for me. And you've likely done the same at some point in your life. It often isn't until we learn how to reawaken our dormant abilities and evoke these mystical experiences that we remember they happened naturally in our younger years.

As you reawaken your spiritual abilities, you may come to realize that some of your childhood memories contain genuine interactions with the spirit world or other remarkable experiences that you had long forgotten. This was the case for me. It wasn't until I started accessing my mediumship abilities as a teenager and began seeing orbs floating above my bed, witnessing a spirit visiting me as a neon-blue energy in the shape of a person at night-time, and waking upright in bed mid-conversation with two people who 'weren't there,' that I remembered I had frequently experienced those things in my childhood too. That realization was the first true sign that the abilities I was activating had actually always been within me. They had simply gone unused for so long. Stored in the back of my brain in the 'Childhood nonsense' category.

I had completely forgotten these occurrences, as they had happened during the period when my imagination was running wild. I once believed that witches were coming through a portal beneath my bed to tickle me, and cast spells on me too.

In those early years, we aren't given the tools to understand what holds genuine meaning and what is a mere creation of our mind. So, when we reach an age when we recognize that our imagination has fabricated many things, we begin to disregard all experiences of that nature. When I 'grew up' and realized that the witches had been a figment of my imagination, probably inspired by a spooky movie or book, my brain categorized everything from that time under the same label. The tickle witches, the orbs on the ceiling, the neon-blue man, the two spirits I used to speak to – all disregarded at once.

> **There's a very strong parallel between authentic spiritual experiences and a highly active imagination.**

When one shuts down, the other goes with it.

This happened to me. The switch was flicked off, and I began operating in 'the real world.'

Without guidance or significant knowledge about the process from a guardian, most people go through a similar experience in childhood, which causes their innate intuitive abilities to fade into the background.

Through obtaining a deeper understanding of how this process works, parents can assist them in deciphering and validating their experiences by staying curious, asking questions, and giving them the space to explore and understand the workings of their minds differently.

But for those of us whose parents didn't have this very niche understanding during our childhood, how do we rediscover those switches and turn them back on?

The most powerful way to reopen communication with the unseen realms is through imagination.

It's ironic, isn't it? Imagination, the very thing we were conditioned to suppress. 'It's just your imagination,' we were told.

But imagination isn't separate from intuition. And when you reactivate it, your openness to the unseen and intangible comes back too, along with one of the most important tools for psychic perception: *inner imagery*.

If you can't imagine a guide speaking to you, you'll never be able to hear one. If you can't imagine a spirit beside you, you won't feel one when it's there. If you can't imagine yourself as a powerful spiritual being, you won't recognize that you already are one.

The way to start doing this is simpler than you might think: start imagining things.

An Invitation

Sometimes the only way to make yourself believe is to live in the world of make-believe!

- Wake up in the morning and pretend that the world is enchanted.

- Imagine your loved ones in the spirit world sitting with you as you drink your morning coffee.

- Look in the mirror and imagine what your own aura might look like today.

- Imagine the fields of energy around other people too. Around animals, around the trees. Everything has an energy field around it, so imagine what it might look like.

- Imagine your spirit guide is next to you on your way to work, giving you some advice for the day or week ahead.

You can do it with anything!

- **The shower:** Imagine a beam of crystalline white energy that cleanses your body, mind, and energy.

- **Your hands:** Imagine conduits of energy that charge your water with the frequencies of peace and abundance.

- **Your writing:** On a piece of paper, create words of enchantment that the universe receives from you.

Let yourself believe that your thoughts are spells, your words are energy, and every step you take is part of a divine unfolding.

Let your inner child run the show for a while. You could imagine fairies in the garden, mermaids in the water, dragons and unicorns soaring in the skies above you in other dimensions. Go to town with it!

You may feel silly at first. And no, you don't need to believe in dragons or fairies to benefit from this. The point isn't whether they're real, the point is that using your imagination reopens your perception to energetic truths. It's the playground where your intuition can come alive again.

It softens the rational mind. It blurs the boundary between 'real' and 'imagined.' And it reopens the very channels you once shut down.

At first, it may feel like you're just pretending. That's okay, because what starts as 'pretend' becomes energetic truth when you give it enough belief. Through relieving yourself of the expectation of what you *should* be seeing, feeling, or sensing and just moving forward playfully, you'll actually begin perceiving energies that are genuine.

Eventually, what once felt like make-believe starts to have a different resonance behind it, evoke a different response from you, and sometimes is even confirmed to be true!

So, as you move forward from this chapter, let this be your foundation:

✦ Nothing has been lost, only forgotten.

- ✦ The abilities you're seeking aren't things to learn, but things to remember.
- ✦ And your imagination isn't a silly distraction, it's the tool that cracks open your mind again.

Trust Where Your Soul Leads You

Before moving on, there's something else to remember.

You may have felt a spark while reading this chapter. A quiet pull. A sense of awe. And just as quickly, a voice may have whispered, 'That could never be me.'

Just like I did, you might believe that only some people are 'gifted,' that spiritual power is reserved for a chosen few. But the truth is: Every soul carries intuitive intelligence and divine power.

That includes you.

And this part is important: The act of putting someone on a pedestal because of what they embody is the very thing that blocks you from embodying it yourself.

When you feel admiration, inspiration, longing, or even envy, you're not just responding to someone else's power, you're being shown your own potential. Your soul communicates through resonance. It shows you what already exists within you by stirring it awake.

So the next time something lights you up, don't shrink from it. Don't let that voice talk you out of what's rising within. Shift your inner dialogue from:

- ✦ 'That's their gift' to 'That's awakening in me too'
- ✦ 'I wish I could do that' to 'My soul is showing me who I really am'
- ✦ 'They're more gifted' to 'That's inside me or I wouldn't recognize it'

The things that light you up aren't just wishful thinking, they're soul-guided instructions.

What you admire in others and wish to have for yourself isn't out of your reach, it's something that you're being called to discover within yourself.

So, ask yourself honestly:

- ✦ Have you already decided that some things just aren't meant for you?
- ✦ Have you made peace with having a small life, believing that greatness belongs to others?

If so, this is your moment to reclaim your truth.

Because the people you admire weren't handed something that wasn't also available to you. They just stopped listening to the voice that said they couldn't, and started paying attention to the nudges from their soul.

You are a soul in a body. That alone means you're already connected to something magnificent.

It isn't out of reach. It isn't for someone else.

It's within you. It always has been.

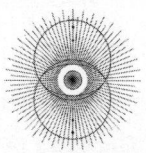

Chapter 2

THE SOUL'S GREATEST BATTLE: THE EGO

We come into this world sparkly, shiny, and pure. Fresh from the spirit world, we naturally carry a lot of our own light within us and are great embodiments of our spirit. In those earliest moments of life, we have no preconceived ideas or judgments. We are simply present – eager to play, experiment, and explore.

Of course, our soul hopes we will grow through each challenge, find compassion or deeper love through every interaction, and expand into more of our own genius and potential through every milestone. However, it knows there will be one challenge greater than any it could have ever set for us. And that challenge is one that no single person gets to skip: the challenge of taking on an ego mind.

In cartoons and movies, we sometimes see that character with mini versions of themselves on each shoulder; one depicted as godly or angelic, the other as devilish. One is a positive influence, the other a negative one. In this reality, we too have two voices guiding us at all times: the voice of our higher self – the soul – and the voice of the ego. But unlike the typical portrayal, where the 'bad' influence tempts someone to do 'wrong,' the ego's poison predominantly lies in blocking us from living out the curriculum that our soul came here to proceed through.

The ego stands in the way of every spark of inspiration and motivation that is leading us toward the greatness that our soul came here to embody. It tricks us into materialism and superficial tendencies that give us a fleeting sense of fulfillment or power. It puts us up against the world around us, makes us feel territorial, certain that there isn't enough to go around. It makes us feel that we must build a pile of goods or resources to sit on.

That pile of materialistic accumulation is the ego's throne, and it wants to die upon that throne. When it successfully makes a person prioritize the material and superficial in their life while neglecting the nourishment of their soul, they end up sitting on their pile of shiny things, feeling the most disappointing sense of emptiness.

And here's the thing with that ego trip: you don't get to make it out of here with any of your belongings. You don't get to take your fancy cars or Birkin handbags with you.

The only things you make it out of here with are your memories. The lessons you learned. The love that you shared. The connections you developed. The elation and pride of manifesting and achieving your dreams. The knowledge you obtained along the way. Those are the only things that truly hold any importance for your eternal self. Nothing else matters.

And this is something that people often have to die to truly be able to learn.

'I should have spent more time with my loved ones.'

'I should have taken that trip to the place I always dreamed of.'

'I shouldn't have worked so hard.'

'I should have followed my dreams.'

These are frequent messages that have come through from the spirit world during my mediumship readings. I've yet to have a spirit come through and say:

'I should have owned more belongings.'

'I wish I'd had a facelift.'

Our ego is something that we develop as a natural response to existing within this world as a complex and intellectual being. As a baby, we rely entirely on others for survival. As we grow and become more self-sufficient, our ego emerges as a tool to protect us and keep us physically safe. It helps us navigate this world, assess our surroundings, and recognize potential dangers.

However, as we have seen, this process leads to suppressing our soul's power and disconnecting from our divine nature.

The soul's greatest challenge in this life is to remain connected to the truth of who we are while living in a world that constantly conditions us to forget.

And the ego is the voice that drives that forgetting.

As we get older, the ego's role expands beyond basic survival and reflects in a myriad of different complex and (often) inconvenient ways. It shapes our sense of self and determines how we perceive ourselves in relation to the world. It's the main driver of our thoughts and emotions – and therefore our behaviors too – and it's what creates the sense of separation between ourselves and anything outside of ourselves. It's what makes us seek validation or praise, or feel the need to be seen in a certain light by others. It can very easily manifest as self-doubt, -criticism, -judgment, -comparison, or the need to be 'right,' all of which reinforce independence and separation.

As the ego begins to step further into the 'driver's seat' and our childlike demeanor fades, instead of being filled with trust, we learn to be doubtful and skeptical. Instead of being optimistic and inquisitive, we become careful, stubborn, and sometimes cynical. That's why it's the ego that is responsible for flicking off those switches we just explored in the last chapter.

Over time, our fearless childlike freedom and ability to be ever-present is overpowered by this new structure of critical internal and external analysis. Essentially, through becoming more developed in our human self, we leave less space within our being for our soul self to remain as present.

The ego is a very intricate and challenging part of ourselves to understand, but our relationship with it is the most important thing to influence when seeking spiritual evolution and the re-emergence of our spiritual power.

In many ways, learning to access your divine power and embody your soul's potential is about *un*learning the ways the world has conditioned you to be through the development of your ego.

Rebecoming the Way You Were

That explorative, inquisitive, and playful nature we all have as kids is one that keeps us aligned and open to the potential of miracles. Getting back to that is also one of the biggest challenges that many stubborn adults face when attempting to access their own spiritual power once again. Once that ego has taken hold, it can be very tough to regain control of it.

There's a common misconception that the goal should be to try to defeat, remove, or somehow disassociate from your ego. However, to transcend its downsides, you must find the balancing point where it can harmoniously coexist within the same space as your higher self.

Your ego isn't your enemy, it's more like a naughty puppy that needs to be trained. But instead of training it to not pee on the floor, chew up your shoes, or bark at the neighbors, you're training it not to minimize the way you perceive yourself or your reality, keep you trapped within familiarity, or make you feel inadequate or unworthy.

Those common traits of the ego are the reason why it can often stop you from taking soul-led steps in your life. When your soul guides you toward something, it tells you through resonance – through that inner spark igniting. However, alongside that feeling of excitement comes the voice of doubt, fear, and excuses for not taking those steps. A voice that tells you all the reasons why you should just keep things as they are, within comfort and familiarity.

That is the ego's voice doing everything in its power to fill you with a sense of security and safety amid your underlying discontent. In its way, it's just trying to keep you safe. It will tell you to 'be realistic' and will make it seem that the things you dream of are ridiculous. It'll try to stop you from expanding beyond the realms of possibility and keep you from exploring the unknown.

Soul Self versus Human Self

Your soul will always act out of inspired joy and ease, and will never lead you down the wrong pathway, yet your ego will do a brilliant job of convincing you to be afraid of that very pathway.

Your soul knew that in coming into this kind of life experience it would take on these constant challenges from the ego. They're the most certain side-effects of human incarnation. In any given moment, you are operating out of the combined efforts of your soul self and your human self, somewhere on a scale between 'in your humanness' and 'in your soul,' and that moment is incredibly transient.

When you're feeling anger, guilt, shame, or fear, you leave minimal space for your soul to remain the predominant force. When you're distrustful, cynical, or judgmental, you are once again disconnecting yourself from your divine nature. But when you embody the innate qualities you had as a child – openness, presence, playfulness, and wonder –

and when you're in awe of life, the light of your soul shines through. And your spiritual power rises with it.

Through keeping your ego in check, you create more space within your being for your soul to remain a predominant force. It's quite simple: by bringing more fun, openness, curiosity, and trust into your life, you create space for your soul to weave miracles into your reality.

Personifying the Ego

Understanding the ego in theory is one thing. But meeting it in your own life and confronting it in the most honest and vulnerable ways is where the transformation begins.

To rewire the way your ego interacts with you, you must first learn to catch it. I like to use a playful, lighthearted approach. I give my ego a name. That way, when it acts out, I know exactly who I'm dealing with.

For example, you may call your inner saboteur Brenda. Brenda is the voice that says, 'Don't try that,' or 'That's ridiculous,' or 'What will people think?' When she pipes up, all you need to do is say, 'Okay, Brenda. Not today.'

It might help to picture your ego. Maybe it's a frazzled, tired, pessimistic, or chronically stressed version of yourself. Give it a face. Then get curious. Talk to it.

When that voice of doubt shows up, ask:

✦ What are you afraid of right now?

✦ What are you trying to protect me from?

Your ego is never trying to ruin your life – it's trying to keep you safe. But it's usually working with outdated information. Let it have its say. Let it throw its little tantrum.

Then invite your soul to speak by asking:

- What does my soul say about this?

- Why has my intuition brought me to this moment?

- If I weren't afraid, what would I know to be true?

Your soul's voice will sound calmer. Wiser. Kinder. Your soul won't shout like the ego does. But its words will feel like truth.

The more often you choose to listen to that voice, the more space you create for your soul to lead. The ego doesn't disappear. But it does lose control. And that's when you begin to access your true power.

> 'Remember, you have been criticizing yourself for years and it hasn't worked. Try approving of yourself and see what happens.'
>
> Louise Hay

Keeping the Stream Clear

There was one very personal lesson I learned in the unfolding of my spiritual connection, one that changed everything forever. It triggered the most profound awakening and transformation I've experienced to this day.

The greatest hindrance the ego poses to our spiritual power is its tendency to shape us into someone we're not. The truth behind the phrase 'Authenticity is power' is one that's often overlooked, yet it's everything. To access your spiritual abilities and to truly harness your soul's power, you must become the fullest, truest expression of yourself. You have to let the essence of your soul pour through you, unfiltered and unrestrained. But this can't happen behind walls, masks, or façades – a truth I had to learn the hard way.

After my encounter with Debbie, the medium who told me about my spiritual potential, I threw myself into my development. I read every book, watched every documentary, practiced every exercise. I worked hard. And yes, I made progress, but nothing felt even close to what Debbie had predicted for me. The path she had described didn't seem to match the trajectory I was on.

I was having occasional profound spiritual experiences, but they were inconsistent. They felt scattered, sporadic, and outside of my control. I couldn't understand why the connection was still feeling blocked.

At the same time, I was carrying a weight so heavy it dulled every part of me. Shame. Anxiety. A desperate effort to hide parts of myself I didn't believe would be accepted by the world.

I was pushing hard for spiritual growth, foot flat on the accelerator, wondering why I wasn't getting anywhere, and not realizing the handbrake was still on. And I was the one holding it there.

Then, at 18, everything changed.

As a Kylie Minogue-obsessed child who preferred Fashion Polly dolls to toy cars, you'd think I skipped the closet altogether. But my ego had fought hard to keep that truth buried. Then the wall I had spent years carefully constructing around myself, trying to appear a certain way, trying to suppress the truth about my sexuality, came crashing down.

The moment I released that burden, something incredible happened: my spiritual abilities surged with real power. My connection to Spirit became undeniable, seemingly overnight. Spirits were showing up so vividly for me that I was telling customers at the café where I worked, who was hanging around them in the spirit world, while they were just trying to order their coffee!

As inappropriate as it was, I was lit up. The floodgates had opened and suddenly I could do with ease what I'd been struggling to do for years. I'd spent so long trying to open this door, never realizing I was the one holding it shut – trying to fix something that was never broken to begin with.

This was the missing piece in all the books I was reading: that before we reach outward for expansion, we must look inward.

We must ask ourselves, where are we dimming our own light.

Ask where are we suppressing ourselves. Where are we trying to be palatable at the expense of being powerful.

When we suppress our feelings, deny our emotions, or live out of alignment with our truth, our energy stagnates. It can't flow the way it's meant to.

Your soul's power is your life-force. Your *chi*. Your *prana*. And for it to flow through your body powerfully, it needs a clear pathway to do so.

Emotional Residues

Imagine your soul's energy like a stream of clean water moving through a forest. Now picture a branch with dead leaves, representing an unprocessed emotion or trauma, drifting down it. If it passes through, no problem. But if it gets lodged, it starts to collect more debris. Leaves, mud, and sticks all clump together until the flow is disrupted. Then the stream is blocked. The water becomes murky. Eventually, the entire ecosystem suffers.

That's what happens inside us. When we don't fully process an emotion or trauma, it gets stuck. More emotional residues gather around it. Over time, it becomes a tangled energetic mess.

And it's not always about monumental revelations like sexuality. More often, it's in the subtle everyday ways we dim ourselves in order to be liked. The ego thrives on control – on presenting an image that feels safe and acceptable. But in doing so, it suffocates the soul's expression. It prevents our essence from being felt by ourselves and others, and the energy that was always meant to flow freely through us gets trapped.

This shows up as anxiety, numbness, reactivity, fatigue. It throws off the nervous system. Every ignored emotion becomes something the body holds as unresolved energy. And as the nervous system slips into survival mode – fight, flight, freeze – the soul's energy can't move. The banks of the stream harden. The flow weakens. We feel disconnected, overstimulated, uninspired, or flat. And no amount of meditation, intention-setting, or calling in the light can override that.

Facing the Blockage

Your soul's power is your life-force. But no matter how divine that power is, it cannot override the blockages you refuse to face. You cannot bypass the congestion and expect the water to run clean. It just doesn't work that way.

To access greater spiritual power, you have to sit with the discomfort. It may not be easy, but you have to fully acknowledge what's been suppressed, consciously or unconsciously, and meet it with honesty and love.

We've seen, through pioneers like Louise Hay, that illness often originates in the emotional body. Sickness and disease very often correlate directly to one of our energetic blockages.

Pain, trauma, unresolved emotion – they all stick. Until they're fully felt, they don't leave. And when we carry that weight, our nervous system stays dysregulated, and we cannot find coherence amid the chaos.

Arguably the most vital step to moving into your spiritual power is this:

> **Relieve yourself of the heaviness you carry. Create the space for lightness.**

This path isn't just made of love, light, rainbows, and unicorn farts – it requires grit. It takes courage to face the darkness, to walk through it, and come out brighter on the other side. It's messy. And the ego won't like it. Especially if it involves breaking down a wall that it's spent years building. But true soul embodiment doesn't come from pretending everything is beautiful while ignoring the build-up in the stream. It means stepping into the murky water, clearing what's stuck, and letting everything move again. That's where real transformation begins.

And here's what's incredible: When you finally address the core blockage – that original piece of debris that caused the build-up – everything caught around it is often released too. When the dead branch is cleared, the water rushes through. Your energy moves. Your life-force flows again.

The shift can be miraculous, just as it was for me when I finally released the blockage regarding my sexuality. It allowed so much life-force energy into my vessel that my connection with the spirit world amplified miraculously. Once I released that guilt, shame, and self-rejection, my soul energy surged back to life!

Authentic self-expression is the very thing that allows your soul energy to rise to the surface and radiate throughout your entire being. When you live authentically, when you stop adjusting yourself for the comfort of others, your energy field transforms. You become a magnet for soul-aligned relationships, opportunities, and experiences. You glow. Your eyes shine more brightly. There's a spark in you that others can't help but notice. That's what happens when the stream runs clear.

The path to spiritual mastery isn't just about reclaiming your abilities, it's about reclaiming yourself. Your power has been within you all along. It may have just been buried beneath conditioning and suppressed emotion.

Harnessing your spiritual connection isn't about what you know. It's about how deeply you feel. How honestly you live. And how courageously you're willing to show up as your truest self.

No masks, no edits, no apologies.

Because the greatest act of self-love is to become the most authentic and fully expressed version of yourself. When you do, the stream flows freely, and everything – yes, everything – begins to thrive.

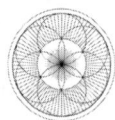

STEPPING OUT OF HIDING AND INTO YOUR FULLNESS

Before moving forward, give yourself the space to reflect deeply and honestly on your life. This moment is for you to reconnect with the real essence of who you are.

1. Sit in stillness, breathe into your heart space, and ask your soul to speak to you. Let these questions guide your reflection or journaling:

    - Where in your life do you dim your light to feel safe, accepted, or unnoticed?
    - When did you start believing you had to hide parts of yourself to be loved?
    - Do you truly believe you are powerful? Why or why not?
    - Where does your inner saboteur still have control over how you show up in the world — and what would it look like to take your power back?

    Let whatever arises be met with compassion, not judgment.

2. Once you've brought this awareness to the surface, take a moment to declare your liberation from unhealthy patterns. Make a promise to yourself, a commitment to honor your truth, embrace your light, and show up in the world as the most fully expressed version of yourself. Say aloud:

    'From this moment forward, I choose to _____'

    Allow your answer to be real, raw, and soul-aligned. Speak to yourself as you would to a beloved best friend or family member.

3. Write it down. Keep it somewhere you can revisit whenever you feel the need — whenever your ego tries to pull you back into hiding. Let it become your anchor, a reminder that your authenticity is your power, and the greatest act of self-love is to live as your truest self.

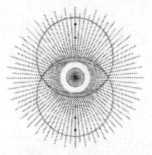

Chapter 3

THE SOUL'S JOURNEY TO EARTH

To harness the power of your soul, you first need to know where to find it. And spoiler alert: it's not hiding somewhere inside your chest, waiting to be released when your body takes its last breath.

The truth is that the vastness of your consciousness could never be bottled up into a human body. So, the process of incarnation is far more intricate than a soul 'entering' and 'exiting' a body. It's far more profound than that.

Many of our collective ideas about the soul and the nature of the spirit world have been shaped by films and television. Ghostly figures floating around and souls trapped inside bodies until death sets them free are common threads, but not ones that reflect the true reality of what we are.

Don't get me wrong, I like *Ghost Whisperer* and *Casper* as much as the next person, but they aren't exactly reliable sources for understanding the nature of our existence.

What if I told you your soul had never technically left the spirit world? That the greater part of you was still there – unchanged, in its fullness, as it had always been.

Through my experiences with Spirit, I've come to understand that the soul never fully leaves the place from which it comes. Rather than a soul 'entering' a body and departing at death, incarnation is more like focusing a beam of consciousness on a specific point within this physical, lower-vibrational reality. It is the process of a soul temporarily minimizing its awareness into a focal point of physicality.

So, you are an extension of your soul. And you simply cannot experience the entirety of who you truly are on a soul level while you're here in this physical form. In a way:

> You don't have a soul.
> Your soul has a You.

The Reincarnation Process

As a soul prepares for a lifetime, it focuses itself upon the material manifestation of life (its future body) that is its intended location. Although it remains within close proximity throughout the process of a pregnancy, it is only upon the first breath that it truly moves its awareness from the spirit state into physical existence.

And that is because breath is what allows the spirit to move through a physical body.

Once that focal point has been established, the soul remains there until the body is no longer able to sustain life. When the breath stops, the connection with the body is severed. And at that point, the soul returns to its original state. It's a process of retracting and expanding, rather than one of 'entering and exiting,' as is more commonly perceived.

The soul never really leaves the spirit world – it extends itself into this realm much like a ray of sunlight shining through a window.

The light is here, but its source remains where it always was.

People who believe in an afterlife often feel that when their time to transition there comes, they will be stripped of their body and mind, and left only with what remains – just one part or fraction of how they're experiencing themselves to be now. However, to call upon the power of your soul, you must understand that you aren't summoning simply one aspect of yourself, hidden somewhere within, you're calling upon a far *greater* part of yourself – a part of yourself that you must *expand into*.

> **On your return to Spirit, instead of being the ray of light shining through the window, you once again become its source.**

To experience life as a human, or any other physical incarnation, your consciousness refracts, directing a portion of itself into this reality. But the greater part of you remains in the spirit world, unchanged, existing in its fullness, as a spark of divine consciousness.

To help fully understand this, consider what happens when you fall asleep at night: your body remains in bed while your awareness shifts into another realm of experience. In your dreams, you move through different spaces and scenarios, have conversations, and feel emotions as if they are entirely real. You have no reason to believe otherwise, as that's what you're experiencing. But when you wake up, you realize that the world you were just immersed in was *never entirely real at all*. Your greater awareness was always beyond it, you just forgot during the time that you were there.

Spirit has shown me that incarnation works in a similar way. The soul, vast and boundless, extends an aspect of its awareness into this human reality, experiencing itself through the lens of a physical incarnation. But just as your body remains in bed while you dream, your soul remains in the spirit world while you live out this human journey. The focal point of your awareness may be here, but the greater part of you has never left its original state of being.

The Power of Awakening

You may have heard of lucid dreaming – the phenomenon where a person realizes that that they're dreaming while they're dreaming. You may have even experienced it yourself. In that moment of awareness that you're currently in a dream, you're able to gain control over the dream's direction, adjusting the scenario or your actions within it.

In the same way, when you become an embodiment of the understanding that you're a soul experiencing a human incarnation, you begin to regain access to your spiritual power.

Just as you awaken within a dream, you awaken within this human life.

You're reminded that reality is quite fluid and can be shaped by the amount of awareness that is brought to it. You remember that you are not your body or your mind – that those are just vessels you're experiencing yourself through temporarily. The greater part of you, your soul self, exists beyond the confines of this physical experience.

Through this remembrance, you begin to experience more of the power that has always been within you.

You also access and embody more of the part of you that remains within the spirit world. When people access their 'higher self,' they are tapping into this aspect of themselves – an expanded level of their own consciousness that remains in its original form.

Embodying Your Divine Self

The spirit world, the place from which we come and to which we will one day return, exists only within the highest of frequencies. Spirit is pure and cannot be tainted; it cannot be damaged or tarnished, and it cannot experience itself within lower realms of frequency without using a vessel.

At any given moment, we are only embodying a certain percentage of this pure and divine part of ourselves. This percentage fluctuates depending on our state of being. When a person carries more of their own light, they are more connected to their spiritual power and operate within a larger realm of potential. Which is the journey you're on: to become a vessel through which more of your own light can move.

Have you ever met one of those people who walk into a room exuding brightness and beautiful energy in a way that simply cannot go unnoticed? People are magnetized toward them, often not knowing why. Those people are embodying a great amount of their own light. And everyone can feel it. And whether they know it already or will do soon, they have accessed great spiritual power.

Mind, Body, and Energy

Since we are souls experiencing life through physical form, our being is currently a combination of *mind*, *body*, and *energy*, and the way these three aspects blend together determines our overall frequency, and therefore the degree to which we're embodying our soul at any given moment.

Mind, body, and energy are each a gateway to accessing our light, and when working together in harmony, they create the space for our soul to fully shine through.

When we're in high spirits, feeling joyful, inspired, or at peace, we naturally embody more of our soul's energy. When we're in lower states of being, experiencing fear, doubt, or suffering, we embody less.

When the ego dominates, there's less room for soul. When the body is neglected, the vessel becomes cloudy. But when the *mind* is clear, the *body* is nourished, and *energy* is nurtured, the soul power flows freely.

Spiritual attunement and advancement come when we consciously balance our mind, body, and energy in a way that favors our connection to our soul. This balance is what creates the conditions for spiritual expansion.

When our soul becomes predominant, our frequency rises, and we become closer to our divine self and all its power.

Your Over-Soul: All the Other Expressions of Yourself

Another one of the questions I'm constantly asked about the spirit world is this: 'What if by the time I return to the spirit world, my loved ones have already reincarnated into their next life?'

It's a genuine fear – what if the people we love most aren't there waiting for us when we cross over?

But the answer is simple and reassuring: the reunion happens regardless of whether a soul is currently incarnated or not.

I came to understand this in the most unexpected way – through remembering my own most recent past life. It was this memory that unlocked something profound within me. In that moment, the nature of incarnation made itself clear in a way I'd never quite grasped before. And the revelation was both simple and revolutionary:

You only live once.

But your consciousness lives many times.

The memory arrived as a vision. In it, I was a baby, lying in a cot. I saw a figure moving toward me. It was my grandmother. But I saw her in the way I'd only ever known her from old photographs – as a young woman. It seemed she was now my mother.

As the vision continued, I flashed forward – no longer in a cot, no longer on Earth. I was in the spirit world. Watching from above, I could see the grief I'd left behind. I felt it. Especially the heartbreak in my (then) mother....

In this moment of soul recall, I remembered making a decision: *I'm going back.* What I had come to do had not yet been completed.

This remembrance came with such clarity, such knowing, that it left no room for doubt. And when I reflected on my own life and that of the baby my grandmother had lost, I realized there were many parallels. One in particular stood out: my name and his differed by just one letter. His name was Dean.

My grandmother and I have always been especially close. Growing up, I spent extended periods of time with her. When I was too young to travel with my parents and sister, Briarly, I stayed with her, and she often joked that she didn't want to give me back to my parents. A deep bond was formed in that time, one that would have mirrored the bond she had shared with the son she'd lost.

Upon this memory returning to me, something extraordinary happened: I felt his presence. He came forward as a spirit, communicating with me in the same way I perceive others in my readings. It was unmistakable. But how could this be? I had just remembered that I *was* Dean. How could he now be coming to me?

He gave me the answer as a deep inner knowing: he and I are expressions of *the same soul*. We are *one* and yet we are *individuals*.

I was communicating with another piece of my own soul.

Though we share a source, Dean exists as a unique facet of that source, just as I do. He showed me that when my gran eventually returns to the spirit world, *he* will be there to greet her, along with all her other loved ones. And then when it's my turn, she'll be there to reunite with me too.

In that moment, I saw that she will recognize us as two distinct but eternal parts of the same soul. She will feel her bond with Dean and her bond with me, and at a deeper level she will know that we were always the same.

This opened something profound within me. I understood:

A soul isn't a single identity. It's a collective.

It is a vast, multifaceted consciousness that expresses itself through many names, faces, and lifetimes.

Each of those lives, each spirit, exists as an individual. And together, they form the whole.

> 'What we have once enjoyed deeply we can never lose. All that we love deeply becomes a part of us.'
> — HELEN KELLER

Imagine walking into a room filled with people. Each one has their own stories, memories, personalities, and perspectives. These people are your past and parallel lives. But your soul? Your soul is *the room itself*. It's the space that holds all of them.

Now imagine stepping into that space, the heart of your own soul, and feeling its magnitude. Feeling every thread that ties your lifetimes together. Knowing each life, with its own voice, its own wisdom, its own unique vibration... and yet knowing all are connected, all forming the greater You.

Each of these lives is aware of itself *and* aware that it is part of the whole. And when this current life ends, *you* will join them. There will be a new presence in the room, a new glimmer of light added to the vast brilliance of your soul.

From that place, you will once again remember everything you've ever known. You will feel all the love you've ever shared. All the lessons. All the laughter. All the loss. It will all return to you.

This understanding reinstated for me the idea that what we learn to access when we access our spiritual power is something that is unfathomably grander than how we experience ourselves now. Our over-soul is a profoundly intricate ball of intelligent conscious light, and through perceiving it in that way we can begin to access more of its divine power.

Soul Memories

This interaction with Dean reminded me of one of my favorite TV shows as a child: *Avatar: The Last Airbender*. The main character in this story, Aang, is met time and again by each of his past lives. They come to him, they teach him their knowledge, and they guide him on his journey of discovering his own superpowers, as they each had too. His interactions with them assist him in his own expansion, in realizing more of his potential, and in overcoming the challenges he is faced with along the way. Their experiences become his, and their knowledge assists him on his journey.

In this life, we too can access the wisdom and knowledge we have gathered on other soul journeys. We can learn from regathering these memories and from meeting with the other versions of ourselves.

When you begin to work toward embodying more of your soul's true essence in this lifetime, when you step closer to the fullness of your divine intelligence, you naturally begin to *remember* more of who you are. You begin to reconnect with the other aspects of your existence, the lives you lived before, the experiences and wisdom you gathered in your soul's previous ventures.

> **The more you embody your soul's power, the thinner the veil between you and your past lives becomes.**

And the reverse is also true – when you actively seek to remember your past lives, whether through spiritual connection, regression, or self-exploration, you're reaching *back* into your soul's memories and expanding into more of its fullness. You're bridging the gap between your current self and the all-knowing infinite consciousness that you've always been.

On the journey of a soul's incarnations, memories aren't lost, they're just momentarily forgotten. But as you walk the path of soul embodiment, those memories come back to you.

The Illusion of Separation

The pathway of spiritual embodiment is one of realizing that there truly is no separation. Just as each of your lifetimes exists within the greater sphere of consciousness that is your soul, your soul exists within the vast ocean of souls that make up God, or Source. And as you return to the awareness that you are your entire collective consciousness, you'll come to see that you are also God consciousness itself. There was never any true separation – only the illusion of it, designed for the sake of exploration.

If God, or Source, were a tree, your soul would be a branch, and each of your lifetimes would be stems growing from that branch. Each stem might appear separate, but they would all be extensions of the same source.

The same goes for each of the branches – they might appear separate, but they too would all be extensions of the same source.

Just as your soul expresses itself through many lifetimes, Source expresses itself through many souls. And your soul is one of them.

This is how Source continues to evolve and create – by separating, piece by piece, spark by spark, so that each spark can become aware of itself and embark on its own unique journey. Your independent consciousness was 'born' through this very process. However, you weren't created out of nothing – you were part of something that had always existed and just at some point along the way became independently aware and started your own unique journey as a soul being.

This is the illusion of separation repeating itself endlessly, so that God can know itself through infinite experiences. This is how your consciousness ripples throughout creation. This is how we are, in truth, all one.

Now before I get a little too *kumbaya* on you, the purpose of this is simple: it is to recognize the grand interconnectedness of which you are an integral part. You are that ocean of divine intelligence in a single drop. Without your light, the ocean would be incomplete. It is only through recognizing this that you allow your spiritual power to effortlessly emerge from within you.

God does not exist apart from its creations. It exists through them, experiencing itself through the infinite perspectives of every soul it births into being.

Your soul is a living extension of God's intelligence. A fractal of the infinite.

You aren't simply an aspect of God – you are God, experiencing itself through the lens of your unique existence. And just as God is infinite, so is your soul. It is eternal. It is limitless. And it is always becoming more.

Here is an exercise to help you get a sense of how grand and intelligent your own soul is...

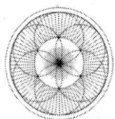

SEEING THE INFINITE SELF THAT YOU ARE

The recorded version of this meditation and others in the book, can be accessed at www.hayhouse.com/download. Enter the Product ID 4724 and Download Code 'audio'.

This meditation will guide you to experience your soul as a unique expression of God, to discover the wholeness that lives within you, and to begin attuning to the many lifetimes and memories, and all the wisdom your soul carries.

- Start by finding a quiet space where you won't be disturbed.
- Sit or lie down comfortably. Close your eyes.
- Take a few deep breaths, allowing your body to relax and your mind to soften. Feel your awareness beginning to turn inward.

Step 1: Connecting to the Infinite

- Imagine an endless ocean of radiant light.
- Feel its warmth, its infinite intelligence, its energy.
- Sense how this ocean is alive – breathing, creating, expanding, rippling through all of creation. This is God consciousness.
- Next, feel yourself as an individual point of consciousness within it.

Step 2: Discovering Your Spark

- Within this ocean you find a single radiant spark of light — glowing, pulsing somewhere within the vastness.
- Know that this is your soul self, the part of you that remains in the spirit world.
- Move closer to it. Feel the love, the power, the intelligence, and the ancientness that it carries.
- The energy that you discover here is the truest part of yourself. It is your eternal self. Your consciousness itself.

Step 3: Entering Your Over-Soul

- As you draw closer, notice that this spark is filled with countless smaller sparks of light, like smaller stars inside a crystal sphere.
- Each smaller glimmer represents a life that your soul has lived.
- Without interpreting or attaching to them, feel the essence of their energy, the richness of their experiences, the wisdom and feelings they carry.
- Allow yourself to sense them as one — their personalities, their journeys, their memories, all woven into the entirety of one eternal being.

Step 4: Meeting the Other Expressions of Yourself

- Allow one of these inner sparks, one of your past lives, to gently step forward. Allow this glimmer of light to transform into the form of an individual.
- Without trying to gather the whole story straightaway, trust the first thing that you sense — a feeling, an image, a word, a sense of time or place.
- Greet them with openness. Meet them with familiarity. Feel their bond with you.

- Ask them to share a memory, a piece of wisdom, or a gift they carry that is ready to awaken within you now. It might reveal something about yourself that you never had a reason for prior to this encounter.

Step 5: Expanding into the Whole

- As you finish connecting with this one lifetime, allow your awareness to expand again, seeing all the lifetimes within your over-soul, knowing you are connected to every single one.
- Feel how all these experiences, all these stories, are reflected within you too. You are the living culmination of your soul's endless journey, and every memory, every gift, every piece of wisdom is accessible to you and will unfold and reveal itself in due course.

Step 6: Returning to the Present

- Bring your awareness gently back to your current self.
- Feel yourself sitting or lying wherever you are, carrying the expanded sense of your true being within you.
- Know that every day, simply by turning inward, you can grow closer to the full remembrance of who you are.
- Take a deep breath. And when you're ready, open your eyes.

Now you have more of a sense of your infinite soul. And yet, to understand it fully, you must look not only at how it operates in your life, but at what brought it into being in the first place. You must come to know the Source that breathed it into existence.

Part II
SOURCE

So far, you've explored the inner workings of your soul. You've come to understand its intelligence, its power, and how it expresses itself through intuition, energy, and presence. You've witnessed how the soul moves through the body, how it battles against egoic limitation, and how it longs to be fully felt and lived.

Now we'll explore your divine origin and the limitless power available to you once you realign with the energy of Source – the divine frequency of creation.

As you read, stay open. Let this part of the journey expand your perception of life, death, the universe, and your own divine essence.

What you're about to discover is where your soul came from and the magnitude of what it is still an integral part of.

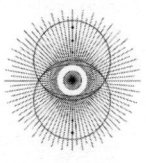

Chapter 4

YOUR TRUE HOME

It's a funny thought, really, that here we are, tiny humans on a spinning rock in space, trying to define the infinite with the same brain that we use to decide what color underwear to wear for the day.

But still we try. It's in our nature to reach beyond what we can see, to seek meaning, to understand where we came from and where we'll go. And through my connection with the spirit world and my relentless curiosity about the nature of this universe, I've received glimpses into the deeper mechanics of existence and the boundless intelligence from which we all originate.

What remains unknown will always be far greater than what can be discovered. But here's one thing I know with absolute certainty: 'God' isn't a man in the sky with a long white beard, sitting in judgment beyond the clouds.

Throughout history, cultures have personified God to make the unknowable feel familiar. It's the easiest way the human mind can make sense of something so vast – by reducing it to something with a name, a face, and a personality. But the moment we filter infinite consciousness through the lens of race, gender, or species, we limit something that was never meant to be confined.

God (or, if you prefer, Source, the Divine, or any other term) isn't a being or a singular entity. It is the creative intelligence of this entire multidimensional omniverse.

God is a consciousness that surpasses the limits of our perception yet flows innately through each and every one of us.

It is the conscious force behind all of creation.

And when I say 'all of creation,' I mean *all of it*. This intelligence isn't just orchestrating our planet, or even just our universe, it's coordinating an ever-expanding omniverse and far, far beyond. It moves through all dimensions, realms, and vibrational densities, of which there are an infinite number.

And the most important part of all this?

That very same intelligence – the force that governs all of creation – is what your soul is made of.

Pause here. Go back and read that last sentence again. This time, let yourself *feel* what it stirs within you. Let it evoke something deeper than your mind.

Now, carry that feeling with you as we go on.

To begin grasping the scale of our own source, we have to zoom out – way out. Imagine an infinite field of intelligent light. A light so pure, so vast, that it transcends all of space and time. A light that holds within it every galaxy, every timeline, every dimension, and every civilization and form of life that ever was or ever will be. This is the creative energy behind all that is.

And your light is a spark of *that*.

That means your power – yes, yours – ripples through all of creation and plays a role in shaping existence itself. Yet here you are, wondering why your latest profile picture didn't get more likes.

You are divine beyond your own comprehension. But forgetting that truth is part of the deal here – it's something you're guaranteed to do, over and over again, while you're on this human journey. Your ego mind misplaces importance and makes you feel far smaller and far less significant than you truly are.

> *'You are the universe expressing itself*
> *as a human for a little while.'*
> Eckhart Tolle

That's why remembering who and what you really are is the first step to reclaiming your spiritual power. Because how can you expect to be guided by, empowered by, or deeply connected to a divinity you haven't even recognized within yourself?

Only through remembering you are that divine power can you begin to experience yourself as a spark of it.

That remembrance is what shifts you out of surface-level reality and tunes you to the frequency that is orchestrating all things. It's from that place that your own creative force awakens and where reality becomes something you shape, not just something you endure. It's from that place that communication with the higher realms opens up.

And the deeper your connection to that truth becomes, the more brightly your own divine spark shines. It begins to shine through you like a beacon, weaving more divinity into the world around you. This is when your dormant abilities and talents begin to be reactivated. It's when the invisible becomes tangible. When magic and miracles move into your daily life. It's the moment you become *magnetic*.

That remembrance is the doorway to the rebirth you've been waiting for.

But while it might sound simple to 'remember something,' it's easier said than done.

Let's look now at what we are remembering.

The Frequency of Divinity

The essence of God as pure divine intelligence can only be described as a *perfect vibration*. Meanwhile, here in our physical form, we live within a spectrum of frequencies that range from very high to very low. We're constantly navigating that spectrum, shifting up and down based on one main influence: *how we feel*.

Our emotions are energetic signatures. While they are deeply personal and layered, we've come to understand their vibrational nature through something known as the *emotional frequency scale*. Feelings like love, peace, and joy have a high frequency. Feelings like fear, guilt, and shame have a low frequency. The higher the frequency, the faster it moves. The lower, the slower.

Within this framework, your *heart* is your emotional center – your tuning fork. It attunes you to different frequencies based on the emotional energy that flows through and from it.

The highest measurable frequency is *enlightenment* – a word that, in essence, means closeness with God. And that's exactly what it is.

The higher your vibration, the more aligned you are with divine intelligence.

Not because God is in a place far away from you, but because this divine presence doesn't vibrate within the low range of physical reality. It exists *beyond* it, while simultaneously projecting itself *into* it. Much like your own soul does....

In other words, God isn't somewhere else. God is everywhere, but cannot be perceived clearly at lower-vibrational states. Divine consciousness doesn't reside above the clouds, but above the frequency of this dimension.

Your soul originates from that higher-vibrational realm. That realm is the spirit world. They are one and the same. Which means that 'heaven,' the 'afterlife,' and any loved ones you've lost aren't far from you at all, they're simply vibrating beyond the frequency you're currently experiencing yourself within.

So is your own soul. So is your spiritual power.

And this knowledge is one of the most significant keys to regaining access to both those things.

Higher states of frequency are the environment where divine energy is easily accessible. Think of it like radio waves. Right now, hundreds of radio frequencies are moving through the room you're in, but you only hear the one your radio is tuned to. The spirit world isn't somewhere far away from you, it's simply vibrating on a channel that's harder to pick up on while you're in this body.

The first step to tuning in? Emotional frequency.

The more you can hold yourself in states of love, peace, joy, and awe, the more easily you become a conduit of divine intelligence.

Connecting with the Divine

It's often the simplest of shifts that can lead to the most profound changes. Connecting with your soul and embodying your spiritual power doesn't always require drastic overhauls – simply living, breathing, and experiencing life consciously can be an embodiment of your divine power.

Sometimes we get so focused on spiritual evolution that we forget simply being alive is a deeply spiritual experience.

You can improve your connection to your soul and the grand conscious force that you come from simply through how you choose to move throughout the world in your daily life. And as with everything else, it begins with your lens of perception.

How you perceive the world plays a huge role in how you feel, and therefore the frequency you emit and align with.

Seeing the Miraculous in the Mundane

The way we see our reality, the way we see others, even how we think others perceive us – every situation acts as a spotlight on the part of ourselves that is active in that moment. How we experience the world around us reflects our own inner landscape. Because of this, we can intentionally transform the lens through which we perceive and experience the world, shifting it to highlight our own divinity and divine power rather than egocentric tendencies like judgment or separation.

Due to the nature of the ego, it's often easier to allow your light to be reflected back to you by the world around you than to try to see it within yourself. This bypasses the ego's belittling voice.

The shift we can make is to move through the world trying to see things through the lens of our spirit.

It starts with letting the world become exciting and inspiring awe within you again – no matter where you find yourself.

You've already imagined yourself in an enchanted world (*see An Invitation, Chapter 1, p.22*). Now...

- ✦ Imagine it's the evening of your first day on Planet Earth. You go outside as the sun is setting.

- You walk past trees. You see birds flying through the sky as it fills with a myriad of beautiful colors – oranges, reds, pinks, and purples bouncing off the clouds.

- Just think how incredible it is to have that experience for the very first time...

- Try to move through this world every day as if it were your first day. Remind yourself of the magic within what has become mundane.

This process is often called 'romanticizing your life' – choosing to see everyday experiences through the lens of wonder and sacredness, regardless of how ordinary they may seem. It's about slowing down enough to realize that life isn't just something to get through, it's something to be present in every moment of.

When you do this, you no longer wait for big, life-changing moments to feel alive. You realize that the way sunlight filters through your curtains in the morning, the sound of rain hitting the roof, the smell of your coffee, the music you choose to play, the interactions you have with others, the way you speak to yourself, are all part of the divine experience of being here. And when you bring presence and reverence to those things, your life starts to feel magical, because you're finally witnessing it the way your soul does.

Many everyday things, once mundane, become remarkable when you pause and truly take them in. No matter where you are, or how many times you've seen something, the more you begin to see the magic of the world around you, the more that magic inside of you rises to the surface.

Start by simply looking up at the sky. It's always there, no matter where you are. Whether it's an endless ocean of stars – some shining brightly enough to pierce the vastness, some that stopped existing hundreds of years ago but whose light is still there to see due to the time it takes for it to travel through space – or it's an endless blue sky with a sun more than 100 times the size of Earth, pouring warmth and life onto our planet, the sky offers ongoing evidence that we're always surrounded by miracles.

Sometimes, the sky is full of clouds, and when enough water gathers, it pours down, replenishing the land, clearing our rivers and streams, and providing us and our land with life's most necessary resource. The moon orbits the Earth, dancing around us and reflecting light in relation to its position to the sun, influencing us and the tides of our oceans with its ever-changing phases. No sunset or sunrise is ever exactly the same. Every morning and evening, the sky becomes a canvas for a cosmic masterpiece, seen only once by those present in that exact moment and location. Everything about the sky is miraculous!

But we so easily forget. The sky is there, day after day, and people don't give it a second thought, or look up even once during their day.

Imagine how your world would change if you could shift your perspective of the sky from *Ugh, clouds again* to *Wow, the Earth's incredible cycle is playing out right in front of my eyes!* That perspective shift is an opportunity to remember how incredible the creation of this world truly is. It's a chance to take something that once seemed mundane, or might even ruin your day, and transform it into something extraordinary, which it actually is, when you stop and think about it.

That simple shift opens the door to perceiving the entire world around you as a divine creation. It aligns you with the grand intelligence that created it all and that you're a part of.

By making these small changes in the way you see things, you begin to remember that every aspect of the world around you is a creation of divine consciousness and to recognize that this intelligence is flowing through you too. You reflect all of that wonder and begin to experience more of it within yourself.

> **When you choose to see things as divine and magical, you begin to experience your own divinity and magic.**

Instead of walking by people on the street and simply seeing someone getting through their day, you remember that they are another eternal spark of divine consciousness temporarily in a human form. You know, when you see a man walking his dog or throwing its ball, that it's a bond that existed before either of their lives even began, that they planned to be here experiencing this world alongside one another. You see every person as divine consciousness experiencing itself in new ways, learning and growing, here to love and experience the wonderful moments in life. You see everyone playing a role in this grand game of life.

When you begin to recognize that everyone else is a divine spark of conscious light, you inherently become a greater embodiment of your own.

The more often you dedicate time to finding wonder, seeing magic, and finding peace, the deeper your gratitude for life becomes, and the more present your soul remains.

Cultivating a deep appreciation for life is guaranteed to change the way you experience yourself too.

See the light in everyone and everything and you will experience so much more of your own.

Making the Mundane Magical

Try incorporating these small but powerful practices into your regular routine. Feel free to adapt and personalize them – what matters most is that they feel authentic and nourishing to you. Then watch how your world transforms.

- ✦ On waking, before checking your phone, place your hands on your body, take a deep breath, and say: 'I evoke the miracle power of my soul and allow it to lead me through this day.' Smile and feel your soul anchoring before your mind takes the reins.

- ✦ As you unlock your front door, pause and affirm: 'I bring harmonious and uplifting energy into this space.'

- ✦ On your way out for the day, see the beauty and soul in every person you pass. Think positive thoughts like *I hope they have a beautiful day*. This trains your awareness to recognize the light in others and reflect it in yourself.

- At red lights or in traffic jams, each time you stop your car, evoke gratitude. Feel the love rising from you and being sent out into the world.

- Every time you step outside or glance out of a window, look up at the sky, consider the miracle of this world, and let it remind you of the vast creative intelligence you're a part of.

- Whenever you choose, sit in silence (even for a minute).

- When you're out for a walk, challenge yourself to notice the magical – a flower in bloom, sunlight sparkling on water, people laughing.

- Anytime during the day, close your eyes and take conscious breaths. Place your awareness in your heart and imagine light pulsing gently from within. Let the stillness recalibrate you.

- In the evening, take a candle and set an intention or make a wish as you light it. Watch the flickering flame and let it remind you of your own inner light.

- During your self-care routine, imagine as you apply face cream or brush your hair that you're infusing vibrant, golden energy into your skin and body. Speak lovingly to your reflection.

- Before bed, dim the lights, place your hand over your heart, and think of three things that brought you joy or beauty that day. Thank your soul for living this day with you.

And if you can't see how truly magical this world can be, then you aren't looking hard enough!

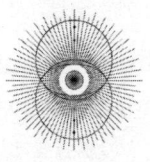

Chapter 5

WHY YOU LEFT HOME

This world is magical, but it's also a place full of suffering, limitation, and pain. One of the questions people often ask is: 'Why would a soul come here?'

The answer lies in the nature of Source itself.

Source consciousness is ever-expanding. And to expand, it must explore. To evolve, it must experience itself in ways it never has before.

That's what creation is – a mirror for Source to see itself within, from every possible angle.

And so, perfection creates imperfection. Not as a fall from grace. But as an invitation to grow.

To exist only in light is to exist without contrast.

To remain in heaven is to never know what it means to return to it.

And so we come here.

Into bodies. Into density. Into confusion, and beauty, and separation, and forgetting. Not to suffer, but to grow, learn, and expand.

That's why you're here, in what I call Earth School.

It's often said that God is the creator of all that is good and that 'evil' or suffering is a result of something separate, something 'godless.' But every aspect of this world, both light and shadow, is an intentional creation of Source. Nothing in existence can ever be entirely outside of it.

As God moves itself into spaces of its own creation, it does so rather like light refracts through a crystal: a single beam of pure white light enters and separates into multiple layers, creating a full spectrum of color, each layer vibrating on a different frequency.

In the same way, as God projects itself into physical reality, it intentionally forms different realms of existence, with varying frequencies and densities, so it can explore and experience itself within them.

This world we walk within is one of those creations – a space where perfection has been forgotten so that it can be rediscovered in new ways.

It's a playground for the grand intelligent light who's curious to become more. And even darkness is an intentional part of the design. While that thought can be confronting, it's also deeply liberating, because it states the truth that no matter where you find yourself, you can never be completely separate from the divine.

Divine Oneness

This even goes beyond this world. Throughout my years of mediumship, I've communicated with countless souls who've lived vastly different lives. Some walked peaceful, beautiful, and connected paths. Others endured hardship, caused suffering, or lived in a deep state of disconnection from their soul. Needless to say, I've certainly encountered some interesting characters along the way....

But what stands out isn't who they were or what they did, it's what they felt at the end.

The way they describe the moment they released their human form is always the same: a complete and all-encompassing embrace of love. A return to blissful, euphoric peace.

You know that feeling of coming home after a long, exhausting day and sinking into a warm, clean, cozy bed? It's like that feeling, multiplied by a million.

> *'Death is like taking off a tight shoe.'*
> RAM DASS

Some of the most memorable messages I've had the privilege of delivering have come from souls who have lived devout, rigid, religious lives. Many have expressed an overwhelming sense of relief – not just because they are free from physical ailments, but because they are free from the fear of what the afterlife might hold.

In that moment of transition, they remember:

+ There is no punishing God.

+ There is no eternal suffering for sins.

+ There is no judgment. No isolation. Only love.

Time and time again, I've heard them say, 'Tell them it's so much better than I ever imagined.' And through them, I've felt the joy of realizing that the fear they lived with was never real. There is no punishment, only growth. No separation, only divine embrace and oneness.

It's a sweet, sweet feeling after a lifetime of internalized guilt and torment.

Ironically, those who approach death fearing God often enter the spirit world with far more hesitation than those who believe in nothing at all.

But the concept of a punishing God is a human-made construct, one shaped in the image of the traditional father figure: the provider, the protector, and often the authoritarian. It was created to keep people obedient and orderly, to control them through fear.

In this time of mass remembrance and awakening, more and more people are seeing through the veil. They're reclaiming their connection to divine intelligence and awakening to the knowing of their own light.

When someone develops a true spiritual connection, they realize they aren't separate from God. They are an individualized expression of that consciousness.

They aren't victims of an external force that dictates their fate. They are creators, shaping reality through their will and creative power.

Religious conditioning often teaches that we must surrender to an outside will. But true spiritual remembrance is the opposite: it's the recognition that divinity is already within us, and that's where our power comes from.

To perceive God as judgmental is to misperceive it entirely. And to experience oneness with the divine is to feel its all-encompassing, unconditional love.

So, whether souls have lived a life of love or hardship, virtue or wrongdoing, they always return to the same divine realm. There are no souls trapped in lower planes. No spirits lingering in suffering with 'unfinished business.' No categories of heaven and hell that separate us based on how we lived or died.

Earlier in my journey, I believed I had encountered 'trapped souls' many times – a mistake that's very easy for a developing medium to make. But as my understanding deepened, I came to realize I was perceiving something entirely different, something void of consciousness.

This is a topic we'll explore in a later chapter. For now, know this:

+ All souls return to their true home.

+ None are condemned.

+ None are judged.

Because everything in this world is here for a purpose. Even the things that seem unfair, painful, or dark – yes, even those – are part of the grand design.

Navigating the Game

As a fragment of God, the soul understands this. It chooses to enter this world fully aware of what it may experience. It knows there will be joy and sorrow, connection and loss, light and shadow. And still it enters. Not out of need, but out of curiosity. With excitement. With love. With the hunger to grow.

It's only once we arrive here that we begin to label experiences as 'good' or 'bad.'

Your soul knew that incarnating meant distancing itself from its own vast awareness. It understood that it would enter an induced state of illusion, in which it might or might not regain full remembrance of its divine origin. But whether that connection was made or not, either outcome would serve the grand experiment nevertheless.

You could imagine your soul viewing life in the same way you would view yourself playing a video game. While immersed, every challenge and victory feels significant. But at the end of the day, the outcomes do not truly affect you, because it was never your true self that was experiencing them. They were just one little blip on the radar, one momentary shift in perspective.

And, let's face it, a game would be boring if there were no challenge or failure. It's only through navigating obstacles that a sense of achievement or reward is attained.

Now imagine that game on a grander scale. For your soul, the real world is the spirit world. A 70 to 90-year lifetime on Earth is merely a moment in your infinite existence. Although your soul is deeply invested in every experience it undertakes, the perspective it holds is vastly different from that of the person living it.

Before you entered this world, you chose the exact challenges you would face throughout your lifetime here – not as obstacles to break you, but as gateways to the power within you. Although it may be difficult to accept, your most difficult challenges, your most painful experiences were choices you made in order to discover new facets of yourself. Every trial, every heartbreak, every significant moment of pain was written into your soul's contract, forged by your own will for the purpose of your soul's expansion and evolution.

And the most amazing part is that your biggest dreams and your heart's greatest desires await you on the other side of those challenges. The difficulties aren't detours, they're actually the initiation. You aren't a victim of the hardships in your life. There is a world of purpose waiting to be found as a result of moving through them – something your human side will always kick and scream about, but your soul has always known.

What I've come to understand is that the soul is relentless in its devotion to expansion. We will sign ourselves up for the same challenge over and over again until we gain the desired understanding and growth. Lifetime after lifetime – if that's what it takes.

From the human perspective, many of the experiences our soul chooses may seem incomprehensible. We wonder why anyone would willingly endure suffering, why tragedy exists, or why some individuals seem to walk paths of immense hardship. But from the soul's perspective, all experiences, whether we label them 'positive' or 'negative,' are simply opportunities for perspective, growth, and understanding.

If this world were perfect, if there were no duality, no contrast, no 'good' or 'bad,' there would be no rhyme or reason to come here in the first place. Perfection would offer nothing new for the soul to explore.

We come here precisely because of the contrast.

This is the realm where transformation, learning, and creation happen.

For many, what I am about to share next is the most challenging perspective to accept. Yet, for those who are ready to receive it, it can be profoundly liberating – particularly for those seeking to unlock their spiritual potential.

Another of the most common questions I'm asked when discussing this area is: 'But what happens to the souls of those who commit evil acts upon others?'

Naturally, as compassionate beings, we're inclined to believe that those who cause harm are punished after death – that the 'bad' go one way and the 'good' go another. After all, this is how our human societies function: We lock the 'bad people' up and keep them away from everyone else.

But by knowing that what we see as 'good' and 'bad' are actually both creations of Source, we can understand why those who lose their way are not condemned. There is no eternal punishment awaiting them.

What we call 'evil' is often the result of deep disconnection. These individuals aren't soulless, they've simply lost touch with their soul. In their pain, they inflict pain. In their disconnection, they seek power in distorted ways. But even in those moments, their essence remains what it's always been: divine light.

They are suffering, however, because to lose the connection with one's own soul is a torment greater than any external force could ever impose.

And when they leave this world, they too return to that same divine place. Because hell isn't a destination, it's a state of being. And it only exists *here*.

This reveals a powerful truth at the heart of everything we're exploring in this book: If hell is the experience of living disconnected from your soul, then heaven on Earth is the experience of embodying it.

We enter this world with amnesia. The aim of the game is to remember. To awaken. To reconnect with our true essence and make the most of our time here.

Some do. Some don't. But in the end, once the game is over, it's over. The soul returns to what it always was, with more experience and understanding under its belt.

This world is the place where the learning happens.

This is where the wheels of karma turn.

This is where debts are paid and gifts are remembered.

Not in the spirit world.

Incarnation after incarnation, lifetime after lifetime, we enter this realm.

And in a sense, we pick up where we left off. We re-enter the game at the level we last finished up on.

Source Connects Us with All

As we were exploring the nature of the divine consciousness that you truly are, you may have felt something stirring deep within you. A flicker of remembrance. A resonance you can't quite explain.

That feeling isn't just a flutter of hope. It's your soul recognizing what it already knows.

We may not always be able to fully comprehend the vastness of the spiritual realms with the human mind, but that doesn't make them any less real. These realms are boundless, layered, and infinitely complex, filled with truths that go beyond the limits of language and logic.

Some of them will never make complete sense while we're here in physical form. And yet, upon returning to the spirit world, every single soul becomes an embodiment of universal knowledge once again.

This is part of the paradox of being human: Your soul knows everything; your mind remembers almost nothing. And you're somewhere in the middle, feeling what you can't always explain.

One of the clearest examples of this disconnect between soul and mind is in the nature of time.

In the spirit world, time doesn't exist in the way we know it. There is no cemented past or future, only a continuous unfolding of being. Spirit has shown me this many times. And while I trust it completely, I won't pretend I understand the mechanics of it.

This is because time as a linear experience is ingrained into our human perception. It's one of the most fundamental ways we make sense of this reality. It's how we make sense of change, memory, and growth. But Spirit has made it clear that time is irrelevant beyond this realm.

Progression, evolution, understanding – these are the true markers of movement for the soul.

Some things will only give you a headache if you try to figure them out too intellectually. It's okay not to know. That's part of the beauty of being here.

The real joy is in being a lifelong student of the universe – open, humble, and always expanding.

And while we may never possess all the answers, developing a resonant understanding of your soul and its origin is the key to unlocking your power.

Seeking understanding of our true origins is not just an intellectual exercise, it's an activation. The pursuit of knowledge can trigger moments of profound resonance, moments when something within you awakens and expands.

That is remembrance of what your soul already knows. And that feeling? That's the very power you're here to learn how to harness.

So, as you move through this book, pay attention to how you feel. Let those moments of inner knowing be your guide. Because you don't find remembrance through intellectual understanding, you find it through resonance. Sometimes, it arrives as a sense of peace. A bubbly feeling in your chest. A subtle shift in perception.

As we've explored, you can never be truly separate from Source. And because of that, you are innately connected to everything it has ever created.

This is what links you to others.

To the universe.

To the omniverse.

To every soul across every time, dimension, and plane of existence.

It's also what makes you a being of remarkable power. It's this connection that allows you to receive information, transmit energy, and communicate with souls on other-dimensional frequencies.

This is what people see as profound spiritual abilities, or even supernatural talents. But truly, it's simply a by-product of soul embodiment. When you're connected to your soul, you're connected to *all*.

To truly activate that connection, you must remember where you come from – not just as an idea, but as an unshakable, embodied knowing. When you remember that you're not just a creation of the divine, but a piece of it – everything changes.

Your sensitivity expands. Your abilities awaken. And the whole field of possibility opens before you.

And in that connection, nothing is actually supernatural, it's simply natural.

But this cannot be taught. It must be *felt*. It must be remembered from within.

You must remember the magnitude of divine consciousness. And then... you must remember that you're a piece of it.

The following exercise will guide you toward just that.

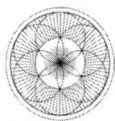

THROUGH THE EYES OF SOURCE

This will help you to perceive creation through the eyes of Source — to remember your place within the magnificent expansiveness of all that is

To begin, find a quiet, comfortable space. Close your eyes. Take a few slow, deep breaths, and allow yourself to settle into a peaceful awareness, grounding yourself to the earth beneath you.

Step 1: Witness the Wonder of the Earth

- Begin by contemplating the vastness of the Earth.

- Imagine the great oceans and forests stretching across the globe, filled with life, from the smallest microscopic creatures to the largest beings ever known.

- Sense the intricate ecosystems, the delicate balances, the beauty woven into every corner of the natural world.

- Remember the ancient ruins, the homes of long-lost civilizations, reminding you of humanity's deep history.

- Consider the vast and busy cities of today, full of life, movement, technology, and creation.

- Reflect on how much wonder exists — and has always existed — upon our Earth alone.

Step 2: Zooming Out — Seeing the Earth from Above

- Now, imagine yourself zooming out, going higher and higher, until you see the Earth from above — a brilliant sphere of blue, green, and white, slowly rotating in the darkness of space.

- See the moon rotating around it in a perfectly synchronized pattern, moving in harmony, magnetizing the oceans and influencing the tides.

- Remember the countless forms of life existing right now on the Earth's surface, each a miracle, each part of the whole.

- Feel the ancientness of the Earth — how old and full of history it truly is.

Step 3: Zooming Out to the Solar System

- Expand your vision again and see the entire solar system — all the planets, from largest to smallest.

- See the Earth's perfect placement — not too close, not too far from the sun— allowing life to bloom across the seasons of summer, autumn, winter, and spring.

- Reflect on how precise it is, how miraculous that such conditions have allowed life to flourish.

Step 4: Zooming Beyond the Solar System

- Zoom further out. See the planets orbiting the sun, the comets, the asteroids, all moving together through space.
- Zoom out even more, as far as you possibly can, until our whole solar system is just a tiny point of light among countless others.
- Imagine our entire solar system as a single grain of sand upon an infinite beach.

Step 5: Feeling the Infinite

- Keep zooming out – further than imagination can grasp.
- See galaxies spinning, vast clusters of stars, endless cosmic webs stretching into the infinite.

Step 6: Remembering the Truth

- And within it all, feel the presence of God consciousness – the infinite energy that creates and sustains every atom, every star, every heartbeat. Know that this consciousness ripples through all that you've witnessed – every world, every moment, every breath, all created from the same source. And you – you are an integral piece of this infinite light.
- Feel the vastness of Source. Feel the immensity of the intelligence and love that created all that you've just perceived.
- Feel how it moves through you as You.
- Sense the truth that you are never separate from it. You are made of it.
- Take a moment to immerse yourself in this heightened state of connection and remembrance.

Step 7: Returning with Expanded Awareness

- Gently bring your awareness back to your body, but carry this remembrance with you.
- Feel the light of Source moving through your being, illuminating every cell.
- Know that every step you take, every breath you breathe, is Source experiencing itself through you.
- Take a deep breath in gratitude.
- And when you're ready, open your eyes.

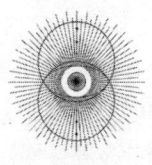

Chapter 6

SOUL FRIENDS: GUIDES, GUARDIANS, HELPERS

In our explorations of this realm, we aren't alone. The idea of magical beings who guide and assist a child from the time of their birth through to the fulfillment of their destiny has existed for centuries. It first appeared in ancient Greek folklore, and by the 18th century the 'fairy godmother' had become a common thread in popular fairy tales. But the core concept – that there are guardian beings surrounding us – has been a shared theme across cultures and traditions throughout time. And it comes from a very real place.

Every single one of us, without exception, regardless of whether we believe in it or have never been aware of it, has a group of souls who walk closely beside us throughout our life. These beings are here to guide us, teach us, and lovingly remind us of who we are, much like the fairy godmothers we grew up hearing about.

Our guides are with us because of a soul connection. They aren't random souls assigned to us by some cosmic order, or strangers that we're meeting for the first time; they're the companions of many lifetimes and many journeys. The bond long predates this life, and we're together now because of a mutual agreement we made prior to coming here.

You trusted your guides wholeheartedly. You asked them to walk with you as you stepped into the divine forgetting that is this human experience.

Through my work with Spirit, I've come to recognize that each of us has one primary guide who remains with us from the beginning to the end of this lifetime. Some call them a gatekeeper or a master guide. These are the guides who assist us as we enter this world and are present to greet us in our transition back to the spirit world at the end of our life. They are the closest to us, our most consistent ally in the spirit world while we're here. In essence, they truly are like our fairy godmother or -father.

At the same time you planned and created your soul's curriculum for this life – its lessons, themes, and challenges – you also made an agreement with this guide, who was chosen to walk the entire path with you, and with others, who were selected to step in at certain phases, assisting you with specific undertakings, lessons, or milestones.

This means that for every major challenge, transition, or evolution, your soul calls upon a specialist from your spirit team to support you. You chose them for their own expertise in relation to that specific theme or undertaking.

Some guides stay for a lifetime. Some join you for months, some for years. Some come in for a single moment in time.

There's no fixed rulebook, only divine intelligence and perfect timing.

You entrusted your guides with directing and navigating on your behalf, but they aren't there to save you, or to force you down the 'right' path. They're there to whisper, to nudge, to leave a trail of breadcrumbs through synchronicity, hoping you'll follow the trail that leads to your highest learning.

Reconnecting with Your Spirit Team

Many people become fixated on knowing their guides by name, appearance, or origin, whether they wore robes or feathers, whether they were Atlantean or Native American. But to put it bluntly, these details are of little significance in our connection with them. They've had many names, many expressions, many faces, many lifetimes. Although awareness of them may come through a visual representation of some kind, the real connection comes through being able to recognize *how their energy feels*. It comes through being able to sense their soul essence and feel its presence.

Often, guides will present themselves in a form that feels safe and familiar. That's why children commonly perceive their guides as 'imaginary friends.' They're not actually children, but show up that way to feel approachable and non-threatening. Our guides meet us where we are, in ways in which we're ready to perceive them. They are conscious, intelligent energy that has taken on many forms. But their *essence* never changes.

That essence is what you've always known. It's what you've felt in moments of deep stillness, inner knowing, or inexplicable comfort. It's what you can feel right now, if you stop and tune in.

Tuning into Your Guides' Essence

When you become aware of your own energy in a heightened state, you can then become aware of the beings that surround you in that space.

Tuning into their energy – the way it feels, the way it moves with you – is the fastest and clearest path to connecting with your guides. Through that, the name they wish to resonate with, a vision of the form they wish to take on and be known by, or memories and dynamics that you've shared together prior to this time, do often begin to be revealed. But we should never focus on meeting our guides through a name or vision, as it stops us from connecting to the thing that truly counts.

And from my experience, we don't get to force these things out of them – they reveal themselves to us in their own timing and when *they* feel we're ready.

It's natural to want to humanize your guides, of course, and these kinds of details do help to give you a stronger familiarity with them, but focusing on them from the beginning can only distance you from actually *feeling* their presence.

Instead, become observant, aware, and familiar with their energy so that you can fall in love with your long-lost soul friends once again.

One of the most direct ways to receive this kind of insight and remembrance is through trance mediumship.

Trance Mediumship

In trance mediumship, the conscious mind of the medium steps aside so that their guide may speak through them, introducing themselves, sharing their wisdom, and revealing the stories they choose to share.

When I wanted to understand more about my own guides, who they were and the ways we had known each other, I turned to trance as my gateway. I trained under some of the world's most respected trance teachers, and when I began practicing the techniques in my own time, the experiences were incredible.

There was one week when I was completely committed to entering a powerful altered state. Every night, I'd sit in my bedroom chair, open up my energy, and invite my guide to step forward and blend with me. The sensations were profound – palpable energy would move through me and the feeling of a consciousness that was separate from my own beginning to merge with me was astonishing. Then, at a certain point, I would 'black out.' It felt like I'd simply fallen asleep. About an hour would pass and then I'd come to, with no memory of what had happened. It was as if I'd simply taken an unexpected nap.

Each night I'd leave my phone's voice-note recorder running, hoping my guide might speak through me while I was in that state. For six nights, there was nothing. Despite the intensity of the energy I was experiencing while initiating the trance, the recordings were silent.

But on the seventh night, the recording was different.

That night when I returned to myself, I felt the same as I had every other night – no real memory, no awareness that anything different had occurred. But when I played the voice note back, there it was: a deep, slow, husky voice. It sounded like an old man.

'Laaaazz... aaa... russss,' it said.

A shiver ran through my whole body. I was in awe. I recognized this voice as the energy I'd always felt within my energy field – that of a wise elder, wizard-like in presence, which other mediums had also picked up on. Now I had a name for him: Lazarus.

His message was short this night, and it ended with: 'I know you've been waiting for me to tell you where and when we've been together before. But I'm waiting... to show you directly. You'll see.'

Believe me when I say he did not disappoint!

Not long after this happened, I went overseas on a trip through Europe. I'd always envisioned Lazarus with me in a lifetime where he was my grandfather but taught me occult practices and mysticism. I wondered if I would stumble across something on this trip that would evoke more of that memory.

It was actually while I was driving through the English countryside with my sister and a friend that he led me to an experience where a shared memory would return to me. It was during a long day of driving six hours down to Cornwall, when we passed a sign for the town of Chichester. Without thinking, I took the exit. Although we'd mentioned stopping somewhere along the way, it wasn't planned – my hands had moved before my mind had caught up.

As we drove into town, strange sensations began rising within me. Once we reached the center, I found myself unexpectedly in the middle of a profound experience.

In the days before the trip, I'd had a vivid dream that I was walking through a rounded, dome-like structure in the middle of a town square. It had archways overhead all the way around. It was night-time in the dream, and I was wearing a long, cloak-like garment. It didn't seem too important at the time – until I found myself standing in that exact place, right in the center of Chichester.

The very structure I'd been dreaming of, which was nothing like I'd ever seen before, was now right in front of my eyes in the physical world.

I approached it and began walking through it, repeating the motions of my recent dream.

As I did so, memories began rushing in. I felt Lazarus with me more clearly than ever and I heard his voice in my head, guiding me.

'That's where you used to live – down there, remember? Up ahead is where you and I worked.'

I followed his voice directing me down the end of the street until I found myself standing in front of an old church. My whole body recognized it.

I stepped inside and the floodgates opened. I re-experienced my past life there – saw myself standing in front of the congregation, wearing robes and addressing a crowd. I saw *him* – my elder, my teacher in that life, in this church environment. We'd run this place together. He'd trained me to follow in his footsteps. I had been his successor.

The memories were so visceral I felt as if I was slipping between lifetimes. It became overwhelming. I decided it was time to leave, but as I walked toward the exit, I got stopped halfway. My feet felt as though they'd been stuck to the floor with glue.

Then I felt Lazarus's ethereal hands being placed on either side of my head and gently turning it to the left. And right beside me, carved into the wall, was a statue titled… 'The Rising of Lazarus.'

He spoke once more: 'That is who I have been most remembered as.'

And then… laughter. A deep, amused chuckle inside my mind. He was having fun with it all.

Trust and Closeness

Your guides communicate with you with remarkable intelligence. They know how much you're ready to know, how much you're ready to remember. They know when to withhold information and when to reveal it. Beginning to trust them, without pressure or impatience, simply through feeling their energy with you, is the fastest way to build a stronger connection with them. When you focus on recognizing their essence first, and trust what you feel, the rest unfolds with divine timing.

Allowing the closeness to occur is the only way to open the doorway to the type of experience I had with Lazarus in Chichester. Your relationship with your guides shouldn't be about what you can get out of them. It should be like all the other relationships in your life – an enjoyment of presence and companionship.

When you learn to recognize their presence, they can communicate with you more easily, whether you realize the thoughts, insights, and guidance you're receiving are coming from them or not. Through the strengthening of that bond, through finding a fondness within your heart for their presence, the stream of communication will naturally open.

Then you can allow your relationship to grow stronger and stronger again, through inviting communication with them in an altered state. Whether you sit in the development of full trance mediumship or simply allow yourself to be overshadowed by your guide, it gives them an opportunity to deliver messages and insights to you with less of the barrier that is your logical mind.

You will have the chance to explore some approaches to this at the end of this chapter.

Rediscovering Your Soul Friends

These beings are the friends of your soul. Among them, there might be souls you've incarnated with before, souls you've guided through their incarnations, companions bonded to you only in spirit, or even other facets and expressions of your own soul. Opening a conscious line of communication with them allows their divine influence to be felt more strongly in your life.

In fact, rediscovering your bond with them is one of the most empowering and heart-expanding experiences you can have. It's an act of rediscovering how much love exists for you that is completely outside of this world that you know.

These beings are the souls that your higher self has decided to put 100 percent faith and trust in during your time on this planet. Just as it chose lessons and challenges, and set intentions for you in this lifetime, it also made agreements with your spirit guides for them to be present throughout. And they themselves are becoming further multifaceted by guiding you in this incarnation.

Building relationships with the soul beings that are there to support you and assist with the challenges you find yourself facing is a beautifully empowering undertaking.

> **These guides love you. They care for you. They wish to see you rise into the highest version of yourself and will assist you in any way they can.**

Being open to seeing evidence of their support in your life allows miraculous moments of remembrance and support to happen.

The key is to become aware of how they feel to you – how they speak through signs, sensations, symbols, and inner knowing.

A Channeled Message from My Guides

After spending years deepening my bond with my spirit team and teaching others how to build their own, I reached a moment while writing this book where I felt that no further explanation, no matter how heartfelt, could match the impact of a message directly from them. There are times when words need to come from the source.

So I closed my eyes, entered the altered state, and allowed myself to blend with their presence. What came through was not just from Lazarus, but from the collective of guiding souls I walk with. Together, they offered a message not just for me, but for all of us.

Here is what they wanted you to remember:

> *We are your friends, the ones your soul has always known as family. We are the warm light on a cold night, patiently waiting to be invited in to remind you of the way back to yourself.*
>
> *We do not interfere. We cannot impose our guidance upon you. It must be welcomed – received with willingness, through a collaboration with you.*
>
> *We reveal our presence in many forms – in totems, synchronicities, sudden awarenesses, revelations, or shifts in your environment. We draw upon the world around you to let you know we are here. We always have your back, and we are always trying to remind you of that truth.*
>
> *Though we may not walk beside you every moment, we are always near the moment you need us. We are not here to hold*

your hand or to tell you what is right or wrong. We are here so you can feel our love and support, no matter which path you choose. We never judge, never criticize, never shame. We simply remind you of what you've momentarily forgotten – and we do so always with the most profound, unconditional love.

We are here to help you see your greatness. To remind you of the desires you held for yourself before you arrived in this body. We are the ones who help you remember your truth in the midst of this self-induced amnesia.

We know you as your truest self. And we know you better than you know yourself right now. And it brings us great joy (and sometimes amusement) to witness your journey through this grand experiment. We learn, too, as we observe your unfolding.

You are not meeting us for the first time. We are the most familiar of companions. We have traveled together through many lifetimes. We have ventured with you before, just as we are venturing with you now. Many dynamics, many expressions, and an infinite universe to explore: we've never run out of ideas for the next adventure.

We are part of your soul family, and you are part of ours.

The ones you love on Earth, your ancestors, and all those who are familiar and recognized by your soul, all are members of this great family. We exist upon the same branch of Source consciousness. And while we may each experience individuality, our growth and evolution are shared.

The soul contracts you entered into overlap with those of others within this family, for the sake of this expansion.

And we, too, are woven into these contracts.

Sometimes we are called to speak, to guide, to show you signs. Other times we simply send our love from afar.

But always, we are here.

Your soul family, your ancestors, and we as your guides are one community, a living constellation of souls that form a greater expression of consciousness.

The miracles we can meet you with there, within that collective, are unmatched.

You may call upon us. You may speak to us. We know when to step forward and we know when to lovingly step back, so you can discover what needs to be discovered on your own.

Whatever level of involvement you feel from us at any moment, trust that it is exactly what your soul needs.

We always act in service to your highest learning, and the way we appear, or don't appear, is always a reflection of that.

Never feel we don't care. Never believe we aren't invested in your becoming.

At times, we may feel elusive, but the truth is we've always known one another deeply, and we can never be out of your reach.

To deepen your bond with us is to deepen your remembrance of home.

We are your soul's neighbors, your eternal kin.

Remember what it feels like to know us this way and you will begin to recognize us once again.

Our love is the truest message we can ever offer.

We are you, and you are us, and together we are something remarkably grand. Together upon this branch, we are the light of a thousand souls. And we all exist within the heart of a profoundly divine intelligence.

So, feel us within your heart. Meet us in your remembrance. Let our loving support reach you, no matter how distant or how near we may seem.

We will never interfere in a mission you came fully equipped to face. But we will always be there, cheering you on from the sidelines.

The rules of this world are sacred. We cannot help you cheat, nor are we meant to. We are here to hold you as you rise through your own becoming.

So hear our cheers, feel our unwavering faith in you, and let it fuel your path forward.

And when you return home, we will greet you in joy.

In that instant, all the love, all the joy, all the ventures we have shared will return to your memory at once.

And oh, what memories we have.

Until then... joyous travels, old friend.

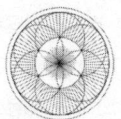

CONNECT WITH YOUR GUIDES

This exercise is for when you're ready to explore a deeper connection with one of your spirit guides and open up a channel for clearer communion.

This is a more advanced process, but it's one your soul already knows how to do. It's a method of allowing a guide to blend with you so deeply that you begin to feel their presence not just around you but within you, as though your energies are merging. Whether this leads into a full trance or simply an altered state of consciousness, the goal is the same: to create the conditions for your spirit and your guide's spirit to intertwine, and to surrender to what unfolds.

You don't need to 'get it right.' You don't need to go deep, feel something huge, or receive anything profound the first time. In fact, the gentlest and subtlest connections are often the most significant. Some people enter a light altered state and feel their guide's energy clearly. Others may simply notice soft sensations, images, or impressions. However it unfolds for you is perfect.

Step 1: Set the Conditions

- Begin by preparing your space for deep relaxation. Light a candle. Put on some deep, resonant music — something that brings you into stillness. Create a feeling of sanctuary. Let your body begin to slow down and soften.

Step 2: Clear and Open Your Energy

- Clear any tension and gently bring yourself into a receptive state.

- Let your spirit rise and your mind sink. Become fully present with your own energy.
- Allow your soul to rise to the surface and fill the space within you and around you with your own light.
- Let your light radiate out as a beacon. This is what will call in the spirit guide who wishes to connect with you.
- Trust whatever sensations you begin to notice. Acknowledge them and allow them to grow stronger.

Step 3: Call Out and Invite the Blend

- As your light fills the space, consciously call out to the spirit guide who wishes to connect with you by saying, in your heart or mind:

    'I invite your presence. I invite you to blend with me.'

Step 4: Focus on Their Essence

- The connection begins through feeling their essence. This is the most important part. Let yourself feel who they are through energy, presence, emotion, and vibration.
- Allow that essence to merge with yours. Allow your mind, body, and energy to be influenced by it.
- If you feel energy moving, allow it. If your posture shifts or your breathing changes, let it. Trust what you feel, sense, or know.
- Begin to feel as though you're becoming that spirit guide.

Step 5: Surrender and Repeat the Invitation

- Keep surrendering.
- In your mind, softly and repeatedly say:

    'I invite you to come closer, to blend more deeply.'

- Continue saying this as an affirmation of your trust, allowing the process to deepen with each repetition.
- Let go of control. Let the blend happen.

Step 6: Enter the Altered State and Receive

- When you feel that you've entered an altered state, where your guide's presence is active within and around you, begin to allow the stream of communication to flow. This isn't a normal conversation. You aren't talking to your spirit guide and waiting for a reply. You are *becoming them*. You may receive images, thoughts, emotions, pieces of wisdom, flashes of awareness, or downloads. Let it all flow through you without trying to understand it in the moment. Simply allow it, and reflect on it afterward.

This is where the relationship deepens – through blending your energy with the guide's energy, and becoming familiar with their unique frequency. The more you practice it, the more recognizable their presence will become.

This opens a channel and leads you to a relationship where communication can occur through thought alone.

Remember:

+ Evoke your power.
+ Invite the blend.
+ Trust the intelligence of your divine light.
+ As you intend it, it is already done.
+ Surrender, and allow the communication to occur.

And if that felt subtle or difficult, that's completely okay. This practice isn't something to master overnight. You can return to it anytime.

The most important step is always *recognizing the guide's presence*. Just saying 'I know you're here and I welcome you,' is the act that opens the doorway.

There's no rush. Your spirit guides will meet you whenever and however you're ready.

Part III
POWER

Through deepening your connection to your soul, everything begins to change. Your energy softens, expands, and brightens. Your inner compass sharpens.

Synchronicities increase. Intuition leads. You begin receiving inner knowings, visions, sensations, and signs from something greater. The invisible becomes tangible.

The world around you reflects the shift within.

Perhaps without even realizing it, you've entered a state of alignment, where spiritual energy is flowing through you more freely than before. The more space you create for your soul to move through you, the more you unlock the dormant abilities that have always been yours. Clairvoyance, telepathy, intuitive knowing, energetic sensitivity, mediumship, creative power – they all begin to awaken.

Life begins to feel magical again. Not as a fleeting high, but as a new normal. You return to a state of wonder, like the version of you that once believed anything was possible.

But this time, you return with awareness. As children, many of us lived in this magic. We felt things. Knew things. Sensed things we couldn't explain. But we didn't have the tools to make sense of it. Now, as conscious adults, we return to that place with clarity, purpose, and power. And with that combination of consciousness and energy, miracles become normal.

You've remembered who you are.

You've realigned with the energy of Source.

Now it's time to learn how to *work with that power* intentionally, consistently... and miraculously.

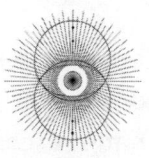

Chapter 7

TENDING THE SOUL'S GATEWAY

If the eyes are the windows to the soul, then the third eye – the pineal gland – is its gateway.

The pineal gland is a small but powerful organ that sits in the center of the brain. Its name comes from the Latin word for 'pine cone,' due to its distinct shape and bumpy surface. Could this be why the pine cone has been revered as a symbol of eternal life and enlightenment by so many cultures? Or why the top of Buddha's head is textured like one? There's far more to this little gland than we have yet to understand.

Throughout human history, advanced civilizations and cultures have revered the pineal gland as the key to spiritual enlightenment. Symbolic references to it are sprinkled through hieroglyphics, religious artworks, and sacred texts, from the staff of the Egyptian god Osiris to Greek mythology to depictions of Hindu deities. Many in the ancient world were in on a secret that modern science is only just beginning to uncover.

The 17th-century philosopher René Descartes famously called the pineal gland 'the seat of the soul.' Today, it's associated with the third-eye chakra, or energy center, which is responsible for clairvoyance and psychic abilities. But when we explore its structure and function, it becomes clear that the pineal gland is responsible for far more than just spiritual vision.

The pineal gland is the center of consciousness in this lifetime. It is the processing hub of our entire energetic field and the anchor point for the soul in the physical body. Structurally, the pineal is incredibly unique. It contains rod and cone photoreceptor cells, just like the eyes, making it quite literally a third eye. It receives signals from your eyes, and when light is no longer present, it begins producing melatonin, the hormone that regulates sleep. When you close your eyes, your pineal automatically begins to activate as your brain shifts to its secondary sense of sight – the inner vision of your mind's eye.

The Spirit Molecule

One fascinating feature of the pineal is its relationship with DMT – dimethyltryptamine.

Known as 'the spirit molecule,' DMT is released by the brain during birth, death, and profound spiritual experiences. It can also be stimulated through deep meditation, breathwork, and plant medicine like ayahuasca.

When it floods the brain, reality shifts, and it's not an illusion or hallucination, but a real inter-dimensional awareness. Consciousness moves beyond the physical into higher-vibrational dimensions, and many people report that the realms DMT takes them to feel more real than this one.

When people say that the eyes are the windows to the soul, what if that's literally true? What if the light or depth you perceive in someone's eyes is a direct reflection of their pineal gland functioning behind them, responding to light, energy, and soul embodiment?

I've had people comment on my eyes in fascinating ways, always at the same moments. Without fail, after coming off-stage after delivering messages from the spirit world, in a moment when my soul is highly present, I've had people say that my eyes look brighter, more vibrant, and more alive. I've come to understand that this happens because in those moments I'm embodying more of my soul's power. It radiates through my pineal and becomes visible in my eyes.

As the pineal gland is the processing hub of our entire energetic field, the degree to which our soul moves through us depends heavily on how well this small but mighty gland is functioning.

One of the most extraordinary pieces of evidence I've encountered that supports this comes from mediumship. Every so often, a spirit will appear in a reading but the person that it belongs to is still alive. This usually means that the individual is suffering from severe cognitive decline. Apart from rare cases like a coma or an out-of-body experience, the only way a living person's spirit can appear in a reading is if their pineal gland is damaged and their soul has begun losing its tether and drifting from the body.

Interestingly, dementia is closely linked to the health of the pineal gland. As the brain deteriorates and memories fade, the soul gently begins to move away from the body. For loved ones witnessing this, it may feel like the person is no longer 'there.' And sometimes they aren't. Their consciousness is already beginning to return home.

But there is a level of comfort that can be found within this: their soul isn't lost, it's simply hovering, wandering, sometimes returning in moments of presence, especially when someone they love is near. The glimmer in their eyes at those moments is the soul drawing closer to the body again.

Calcification and Crystals

Research has found that the pineal glands of Alzheimer's and other dementia patients often show extreme calcification – mineral build-up that hardens the gland and restricts its function.[2] In many cases, the gland appears so encrusted it almost looks like a crystal. No wonder it can no longer perform its sacred task of anchoring the soul to the body.

If a damaged pineal results in soul disembodiment, then a healthy pineal supports a deep level of soul embodiment. And that brings us to something truly extraordinary, especially if you're a fellow crystal lover.

In 2002, scientists discovered that the pineal gland contains microscopic quartz-like crystals with piezoelectric

---

[2] Juhyun, S. (2019), 'Pineal Gland Dysfunction in Alzheimer's Disease: Relationship with the Immune–Pineal Axis, Sleep Disturbance, and Neurogenesis', *Molecular Neurodegeneration*, 14.

properties.[3] This means that they can generate electrical charges when exposed to pressure or friction. You may have seen this demonstrated in experiments where two crystals rubbed together in the dark emit sparks of light. These kinds of crystals are also used in radios to tune into different frequencies.

So, if you're walking around with these frequency-attuning crystals in your head, what does that mean for your consciousness?

These crystals are your soul's receivers and transmitters. They are the point of contact where Spirit becomes flesh, where energy becomes form. They help determine the frequency of your entire field.

When your pineal gland is healthy, blood flows freely through it and the crystals remain charged and active. But when it becomes sluggish, calcified, or clogged with toxins, that current dulls.

To align with your soul's high frequency, you need to keep your pineal clear and stimulated.

Unfortunately, in today's world the pineal gland is under constant assault. As a high-blood-flow, soft tissue, it filters a lot of what enters our body – and accumulates many of the harmful substances we're exposed to daily. Over time, this causes calcification.

The biggest offender? Fluoride. This controversial chemical, found in tap water, toothpaste, and some table salts, binds

---

3   Baconnier, S., *et al.* (2002), 'Calcite Microcrystals in the Pineal Gland of the Human Brain: First Physical and Chemical Studies', *Bioelectromagnetics*, 23(7): 488–95.

with calcium in the body, strengthening tooth enamel, yes, but severely calcifying the pineal.

Other culprits include pesticides, food preservatives, heavy metals, and the synthetic chemicals found in cookware and aerosols. We're surrounded by substances that damage the very gland that governs our spiritual vitality.

But don't worry, you can begin to decalcify and strengthen the health of your pineal gland.

Strengthening the Pineal Gland

The good news is that by combining movement, nourishment, and mindful care, you can restore your pineal gland's vitality – and in doing so, access a deeper level of soul embodiment. Think of this not just as care for an organ, but a way of tending the gateway through which your spirit radiates.

Breathwork

Breath is the first key. Deep, slow, and intentional breathing doesn't just oxygenate your body, it stimulates the back of your throat and your sinuses. Because of their relative proximity to where the pineal gland is sitting, their movement helps stimulate the area, massage it, and activate more blood flow. This goes for anything where your breath becomes heightened.

If you've practiced breathwork, you now know why your internal vision can become incredibly active during your sessions.

Exercise

As blood pumps through your body, it's moving through your brain and pineal too. Cardiovascular activities like gym work, running, swimming, Pilates, yoga, or dancing encourage circulation. Yogis have long known the benefits of completely turning themselves upside-down, allowing blood to flood their heads. Now you know why: Inversions like headstands and downward dog can help flush the pineal gland with a higher-than-usual blood flow and stimulate detoxification.

Meditation

Meditating naturally stimulates this part of the brain. Mindful focus or attention on the third eye will lead to its activation. Flashes of color, especially blue, are often the result of the piezoelectric crystals within the gland being stimulated.

Sunlight Exposure

Sunlight plays an important role in the regulation of the pineal gland. The pineal is highly sensitive to light and directly regulates our circadian rhythm, as well as melatonin production and overall spiritual awareness.

Natural sunlight stimulates serotonin production, which later converts to melatonin, promoting deep rest and heightened intuition. Sun-gazing during the early morning or late evening (although be careful not to look at it directly!), when the sun's light is softer, can activate the pineal gland and assist in its decalcification.

Foods and Supplements

The list of ways to stimulate the pineal goes on and on, and alongside physical practices, there are certain foods and supplements that have been found to be great supports in the decalcification of the pineal gland:

- **Blue Lotus Flower:** The blue lotus was considered sacred in ancient Egypt, a flower that symbolized both rebirth and divine sight. When infused as a tea, it contains natural compounds that quieten the nervous system and deepen intuitive states. The Egyptians believed that consuming blue lotus could open the soul to visions of the afterlife. Today, we know its alkaloids interact with the brain's receptors, supporting relaxation and altered states of consciousness. The compounds are known not only for greatly supporting the decalcification of the pineal gland, but also for stimulating psychic vision, lucid dreaming, and deeper intuitive awareness on all levels.

- **Cacao:** Raw cacao, often called 'the food of the gods,' has been revered in ceremonial traditions across Mesoamerica for thousands of years. Nutritionally, it's rich in magnesium, antioxidants, and theobromine, which all increase blood flow to the brain and elevate mood. But beyond the physical, cacao has a way of feeling like liquid light moving through the body. It activates both the mind and the heart, thanks to its abundance of neurotransmitter-enhancing compounds that stimulate the pineal gland and help open the door to expanded states of consciousness.

- **Pineapple:** Nature often hints at a plant's healing properties through its form and appearance. Red tomatoes and peppers, both of which often have four chambers, mirror the four chambers of the heart and are renowned for their cardiovascular benefits. Walnuts resemble the folds of the brain and are celebrated as a powerful brain food. Slice a carrot and the rings look strikingly similar to the structure of the human eye, which is fitting, since carrots are excellent for eye health. Bananas have been known to be good for... well, you know what.

  And pineapple is no different. Its outward shape closely resembles the pineal gland itself, with its spiky exterior protecting a radiant core. Pineapple carries bromelain, an enzyme known for reducing inflammation and supporting detoxification. It's almost as though nature designed this fruit to be a mirror for the gland it nourishes.

- **Other Allies:** Other supportive allies weave into this picture as well. Turmeric, with its golden pigment curcumin, is widely known for reducing calcification. Apple-cider vinegar aids detoxification and balances internal chemistry. And iodine-rich foods like seaweed not only strengthen the thyroid but indirectly support the pineal gland's function too.

By nurturing the pineal gland, we can enhance our soul embodiment, allowing the full brilliance of our spiritual essence to radiate through our physical form.

The pineal holds the secrets to life, death, and the mysteries of the universe.

This sacred gland is the bridge between matter and spirit.

Protect it. Activate it. Honor it.

And you will feel the light of your soul shining more vividly than ever before.

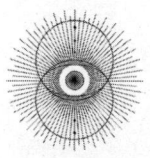

Chapter 8

HARNESSING YOUR SOUL'S POWER

Transcendence isn't about going to some higher plane, it's about bringing the power of Source to where you're sitting or standing, here and now. It's the act of consciously creating space within yourself for that divine energy to manifest. Harnessing that energy is the key to becoming a master of your reality, to living a blissful existence, and to being a conduit for higher-vibrational planes.

Harnessing the power of your soul is what transforms you into a divine conduit of your truest self. This is what unlocks your greatest potential, magnetizes miracles, and aligns you with the life you came here to live. It's the key to your greatness. The doorway to fulfillment. The most direct path to the miraculous.

It all happens through becoming more soul-led.

True fulfillment comes only through soul embodiment. Through filling yourself with life-force energy. With consciousness. With spirit.

Through soul embodiment, the supernatural becomes natural. The miraculous becomes normal. You can communicate with Spirit, heal the mind and body, manifest your most desired timelines, and open yourself to extraordinary realities. And you begin to realize that the life you've always longed for is the life your soul brought you here to experience.

The Expanding Field

Spirit has impressed upon me that throughout our history, as artists and visionaries have moved into an inspired state, they have unknowingly become expansive and connected and, as a result, accurate conduits of the spiritual realms. They have channeled glimpses of the spirit world which have communicated very important universal truths and information to us. It's almost as though the spirit world has sprinkled breadcrumbs within certain bodies of work to assist us in our endeavors to understand how to bridge our realm and theirs.

Although I'm certain that this blend between Spirit and artists happens on an incredibly broad scale, and frequently too, there are two particularly well-known examples that Spirit has highlighted to me. These have great significance when it comes to understanding our connection with the spirit world and, therefore, also with our own higher power.

'The Vitruvian Man'

The first of these examples is Leonardo da Vinci's 'Vitruvian Man,' a drawing that displays Da Vinci's interpretation of a 'perfect man,' using ancient knowledge of ratios and proportions relating to physical human anatomy. What Spirit has shown me is that within this artwork there's a whole other layer of meaning that we're missing. It's displaying a perfection that goes beyond the physical alone.

Da Vinci's 'Vitruvian Man' depicts a perfect human energetic field.

'The Vitruvian Man' contains an element that is not a part of a physical human body: the circle that surrounds the man. Although this may be there to draw attention to the body's geometric nature, it also, perhaps accidentally, depicts a *perfect* human energetic field, a natural conduit for the man's spirit and the higher spiritual realms.

The expansiveness of our energetic field fluctuates, based on the speed of the frequency that is moving through it. That frequency is determined by the vibration of the emotions we are experiencing. When we experience lower-density emotions, our field retracts and moves closer to our body. When we're experiencing sadness, grief, and shame, for example, it surrounds us like a cocoon. These are the times when we're 'in our shell,' protecting ourselves in the heaviness of our emotions.

On the other hand, when we experience high-vibrational emotions such as love, bliss, euphoria, and joy, the energy we're emitting is naturally pushed outward from us, so our field becomes expansive. This is the space in which we're able to connect to all the realms of divinity. We're quite literally expanding more into our own consciousness and accessing a state closer to our Source – 'the flawless vibration.'

Something I learned early on from one of my mentors was that to know where the spirit world is, all you have to do is reach your arm up and out to your side and wiggle your fingers. Where you're wiggling your fingertips is how far away the spirit world is from you. That space physically represents the approximate vibrational gap between our world and that world. (Okay, you can put your arm back down now.) The reason for it is because that's how far we have to extend our own field of energy to be able to interact with that vibration.

In 'The Vitruvian Man,' the circle around him is in the exact place where the energy field would be of a person who was accessing their divine power and being a clear conduit of the spiritual realms.

'The Creation of Adam'

The second example that I've been led to understand is encoded with spiritual knowledge is Michelangelo's painting on the ceiling of the Sistine Chapel of the Vatican, 'The Creation of Adam.'

The touching fingertips in Michelangelo's 'The Creation of Adam' shows the place where we meet Spirit.

On initial impression, this artwork depicts the relationship between God and man. It's also clear that there's a lot of intentional messaging within it. The fact that God and the spirit world are depicted within the anatomy of the brain (*not pictured here*) tells us that this is the area of the body we need to understand in order to connect to them. The shape of the pineal gland is clearly highlighted. But what I see as a more immediately implementable understanding is that the place where we reach God/Source/Spirit is, once again, quite literally at our fingertips.

Of course, it challenges us to try and understand 'where' to find something that isn't in physicality as we are. We have to locate it through vibration alone.

Accessing Your Power

For me, when learning how to communicate with Spirit, the most challenging thing was how to achieve consistency in accessing my power. Often it worked wonderfully – the accurate information felt easily accessible and the words that Spirit wanted to share appeared in my awareness effortlessly; other times the connection felt uncertain, doubtful, and I seemed to be exerting myself to make it happen.

But through trial and error I worked out a methodology that helped me 'crack the code.'

I realized that the times when it was working well for me were when I was excited beforehand. Connecting with the spirit world felt enjoyable and light, whereas in the more difficult moments, I wasn't really approaching it with much willingness, which 99 percent of the time was due to my fear of not being able to connect.

I realized that I wasn't feeling good *because* my connections were going well – it was actually the other way around: my connections were going well *because* I was feeling good.

It was the same with the ones that weren't going so well: their lack of success was down to the energetic state I was approaching them with.

After I had this realization, whenever I was about to practice an exercise and offer a reading to someone, I would first excuse myself and say I needed to use the bathroom. Secretly, I was going to have a moment of privacy so that I could psych myself up. I would jump up and down on the spot while quietly saying to myself, 'Sean, this connection is going to be amazing. It's going to be epic!'

Through this I would manipulate my emotional state into one that was heightened and excited. I would then come back and sit down, open up to the spirit world and start my reading straightaway. Time after time when implementing this, I would bring through a connection with Spirit that left my client with their jaw open. I felt I'd cracked the code to consistently making strong and powerful connections on cue.

I now know that what I was doing in these moments was the very action that these artworks were communicating: I was reaching the realm of the spirit world, and my spiritual power, by expanding my field of energy through influencing my emotions.

Elevating my state of being *before* attempting to do something energetic became a revelation. It brought *ease* where there was once effort, *clarity* where there was once doubt, and *joy and play* where there was once fear and nervousness. Once I discovered this, it was no longer a question of 'Will this work?' but rather 'How good can this get?'

Whether it's mediumship, accessing your soul's divine intelligence, channeling a healing frequency, or calling in a manifestation, it all begins the same way:

Feel good first.

That's the secret. As simple as it may sound.

Spiritual power isn't something you access by trying harder. It responds to who you're being right now.

That's why you can't wait until things go well to feel good. You must *feel good so things can go well.*

This is what ultimately led me to stop quietly meditating before my readings and start putting on some Kylie and having a solo disco party instead! I discovered that fun, play, and joy were the gateways to profound power and easy interactions with divine energy.

When we approach our goals and energetic endeavors from a state of lightness and excitement, we unlock the energy that makes connection, clarity, and success feel effortless.

Our ego makes us take everything so damn seriously. It makes everything so incredibly important that we stunt our own growth and fall out of alignment and flow. Joy, on the other hand, raises our frequency faster than anything else.

Spirituality has often been made to seem like something strict, disciplined, calm, and only accessed through stillness. But that is more the practice of regaining control of the mind. And although that is a very important undertaking, your power finds you in ways that are much more fun than that.

So, let yourself move with ease, with grace, with a smile on your face. Unclench those butt cheeks and stop taking everything so seriously. Because the most sacred preparation for greatness is simply feeling good and meeting it with fun.

A Natural High

Although mediums, shamans, mystics, and other spiritual seekers may have become conscious of how to utilize their soul energy for specific purposes, other people tap into it all the time – without even realizing it.

Spiritual power isn't some unfamiliar force you've never experienced before. It's not going to feel foreign or out of the ordinary when you learn to recognize it. It's something you've likely already felt many times throughout your life.

It's the feeling of expansiveness. Of wonder. Of being awestruck by what's unfolding within you and/or around you. The sensation of being in your spiritual power is a natural high like no other.

Imagine a singer on stage, fully immersed, in their element, hitting every note. Their energy is palpable – it's clear they're doing what they were born to do. At the height of their performance, members of the audience are overcome with goosebumps – a signal from their bodies that something vibrationally profound has just occurred within them. It's all energy. And whether the singer realizes it or not, they've just accessed the divine power of their soul by doing what they love. And whether the members of the audience know it or not, it's something they all can feel too.

The singer comes off stage elated, ecstatic, even amazed by themselves. In that moment, they've accessed their own greatness. They've just accessed the very same energy that mediums use to communicate with the spirit world.

That feeling – that sense of being completely lit up from the inside out, flooded with wonderful emotions, or fully in love with the moment you're experiencing – is the notification that you've just accessed something divine.

It rises in more subtle ways too. It's that flutter in your chest when you speak about something you love, that warm glow when you've just done something you didn't know you could do. In those moments, your soul is moving through you.

It gives you the underlying feeling that you're truly living your life in the way it was meant to be lived. And that feeling is your soul saying, 'This is what I came here for. This is what it's all about.'

Rarely does the ego have a role in that state, other than a healthy sense of pride.

A Higher Level of Potential

Whenever a person enters that space, they are automatically operating at a higher level of potential. And in that expanded moment, what's flowing through them is a powerful spiritual energy – one that doesn't just uplift them and connect them to their soul, but has the power to influence reality altogether. But because most people only ever evoke it accidentally, it tends to flow in the direction of familiarity, following the expectations and beliefs of the person who has accessed it.

But what if you could intentionally harness that power with an expanded perspective and conduct it in a specific direction?

What if it could be consciously harnessed to create new miracles?

This is what mediums have discovered: how to call upon that sacred energy, evoke it intentionally, and direct it with purpose.

For us, the intention is to communicate with souls on the other side. But for you, it could be anything you set your mind to.

Embodied Belief

Your mind is the instrument of direction. So when you're working with this energy, your embodied belief is one of the most essential components of success.

How does it work? Whatever belief you embody becomes real – immediately on an energetic level and eventually on a literal one. So the way forward is to tell yourself that you're capable of what you're setting out to achieve, while feeling it as a truth in every part of your being. Only then do you set yourself up for success in actually achieving it.

In order to utilize this energy to communicate with the spirit world, mediums evoke it and then combine it with the clear intention to open our awareness to communicate with the intelligence of Spirit. Since we've done that before, we're an embodiment of the belief that we're capable of it.

To access our power, we remember the divine nature of Spirit, the infinite light that we are. We honor it, give thanks for it, and allow our reverence to spark the feelings of wonder. We imagine ourselves opening to that light, and in doing so, we *feel* it. That feeling activates and gives momentum to the energy even further. And that's the very process that allows us to perform the miracle of mediumship.

It's all about coherence.

There's a sweet spot where this beautiful unconscious energy becomes a superpower that can be used with intent. It's when we're using our heart as an instrument to elevate our emotional frequency and become expanded within our energetic field, and when we're embodying supportive beliefs, silencing the chatter in our mind, and being clear in our intention.

Coherence within each of these aspects is where the greatest and easiest success occurs. If any one of these things is missing, the equation falls out of balance and the miracle doesn't manifest.

Elevated heart. Steady mind.
That's the equation.

It isn't about perfectionism. It isn't about rigid control or forcing stillness. You can't expect complete mental silence, you can't expect to be completely unwavering within your vibration and intention, you don't need to be flawless – you just need a wholehearted approach, with conscious surrender and loving awareness.

Whether it's calling in a manifestation, communing with Spirit, receiving healing, or simply seeking divine guidance, every experience of an expansive nature can be invited with this approach.

So let's break it down even further, in a way where you can consciously tap into this energy.

The Power Process

Of all the teachings of mediumship, none is more sacred, more essential, or more powerful than what we call 'the power.' This is the energy that bridges dimensions, the vital force that awakens our soul power and allows miracles to move through us.

In other modalities, it's referred to as *chi* or *qi*, *prana*, 'life-force,' or sometimes even 'the force.' Regardless of the name, the principle remains the same: to shift the scales – tame the mind and elevate the spirit – to access the divine within.

It's long been a mission of mine to explore this power in all its layers – to decode it, understand it, and learn how to master it. Mediums have traditionally been tasked with using this energy for their work, but I believe it's time we let the world in on our secrets.

Everything we've explored so far in this book has been designed to support you in understanding and accessing your power in the most streamlined way. Let's quickly refresh the foundational keys that make this possible.

Acknowledging Who You Are

First, it's essential to be connected to the truth of your soul and where you come from. When you contemplate your divine origin and the grand consciousness you're part of, something inside you is evoked. A resonance is formed and your power begins to stir.

Second, it's important to understand that you are not embodying 100 percent of your soul in this incarnation. A much greater part of you still exists in the spirit world. That higher part of your being, the over-soul, is what you're calling into your being in this process. You're seeking union with the divine aspect of yourself, embodying more of its power in a heightened moment.

Sitting in the Power

When you do this, as we've seen, you momentarily allow the presence of your spirit to rise within you and take up the space that's usually occupied by your human self. It requires a refining of the mind, a move away from analysis, and an expansion into blissful interconnectedness and divine reverence.

This is where 'sitting in the power' comes in – a tried and tested practice passed down through generations of devoted mediums. It is honored as an essential practice in becoming a refined and powerful vessel for Spirit, the energetic preparation required to become a powerful medium.

In this practice, you sit with the clear intention of allowing your mental world to settle and your soul self to rise. You consciously evoke the spiritual power from within, allow it to expand your energetic field to the perfect point, just like 'The Vitruvian Man,' and hold it for as long as you can. Over time, with regular practice, this becomes easier. Your energy field expands, your accuracy sharpens, and your ability to work with Spirit becomes more effortless and sustainable.

As blissful and euphoric as this state feels, you can also sense your inability to 'stay there' after a certain amount of time. This is because your body and mind must exert energy to facilitate the manifestation of your spirit.

This process is not dissimilar to physical training. If you were to go to a gym, pick up a weight, and hold it out in front of you, after a certain amount of time your arms would become strained, you'd begin to feel uncomfortable, and your body would signal to you to release the weight. If you were to go back and practice that every day, though, your endurance would build, and over time you'd be able to hold that weight for longer. Eventually you'd be able to choose a heavier weight to hold, because your body would become attuned to facilitating energy in that way and strengthen itself accordingly. The same principles apply to your body and mind in terms of facilitating your spiritual power – it takes training, repetition, and dedication.

Elevating Through Emotion

The spirit world operates at a much higher frequency than we do here, and to access it we must intentionally shift our emotional state. High-vibrational feelings like gratitude, reverence, joy, and love, as we've seen, bring us closer to the miracle frequency. They expand our energetic field and elevate us into resonance with our spirit.

Of course, we don't always feel those emotions on demand. This is where memory and imagination become powerful tools. If you can't readily access gratitude or joy in the present, remember a time when you did, or imagine what it would feel like to experience a miraculous amount of it. Your mind and body don't know the difference between 'real,' 'remembered,' and 'imagined,' and all create the same energetic response within you.

Now, once that emotional state is sparked, support it through visualization to draw a response from your energetic field.

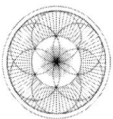

VISUALIZATION

1. With stillness in your mind and belief in your intention, begin by visualizing a small light at the center of your chest. Then allow that light to grow. It doesn't matter what it looks like; what matters is your belief in what you're doing. That belief gives life to your intention.

2. Visualize the light expanding, filling more of your being and radiating outward. Experience it with as many of your senses as you can. Through this act, you're creating space for your divine self to step in and manifest within you.

3. As you do this, you may notice subtle or not-so-subtle feelings arising. It's crucial to acknowledge and validate every sensation, no matter how slight or strong. Little shifts open the pathways

for the energy to grow stronger. Over time, they can evolve into profound and undeniable experiences. But in the beginning, subtlety is everything, so it's key to always honor it.

4. One of the most important parts of this process is often the most overlooked: the breath. Breath is life. Without it, there is no life-force energy moving through the body. Your breath energizes you, oxygenates your blood, activates your pineal gland, and increases your overall ability to harness more of your power. Conscious breathing anchors your awareness and settles your mind. Steady, focused breathing is a crucial element of this process.

5. If at any point you feel stuck, distracted, or doubtful, return to your breath. Let it carry you through this process, amplifying and intensifying every little sensation, feeling, or vision as it does so.

6. When the energy begins to truly build, you won't need to think about the steps above. The process will begin to carry itself. You'll feel waves of light rippling through you. You'll be in awe of your own divine self as it's evoked within you. You'll feel present, expanded, and immersed in bliss. And in that state, you'll be embodying far more of your soul than normal. You'll be bathing in the glow of your own divine light.

And the energy that you're feeling in the exercise above? That's your spiritual superpower. The secret you came here to learn.

The more you evoke it and experience it, the stronger and more powerful it will become.

Don't be surprised if it stirs emotions in you, or even brings you to tears on your first successful attempt to evoke it. I've seen countless people become emotional when accessing this space.

Why? It's a return to who you really are. So, it moves you. It changes you. It's golden, electric, and sacred.

Many describe the sensation as champagne bubbles rising through their torso, or the space around them becoming alive. It's different for everyone, but miraculous every time. You'll move into euphoric ecstasy when you tap into it correctly.

Accessing your spiritual power comes down to one core principle: your state of being.

Everything else – emotion, breath, visualization – is simply a way of supporting that state.

It's all frequency. And any tool that elevates your frequency is a brilliant support to this process. But my own favorite is music.

It doesn't matter whether it's shamanic drumming, electronic house music, or a cinematic orchestral track. These are the types that work best for me personally, but you need to find what works for you. Whatever it is, it has to be what stirs your energy. What you respond to on a vibrational level.

✦ ✦ ✦

Here are the simplified steps to implement when tapping into your divine power:

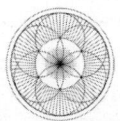

TAPPING INTO YOUR DIVINE POWER

Find your music, settle yourself, and begin taking deep, rhythmic breaths into your core.

- Shut your eyes and become present with yourself. Give no thought to anything outside of your intention and the present moment.
- Invite an elevated state of emotion through imagining an amazing feeling or remembering a moment in time when you experienced one. Allow it to fill you up.
- Consider the true nature of your soul. Be in a state of reverence for God/Source/Spirit.
- Keep breathing as you allow your analytical mind to subside.
- Visualize a small bright light shining from within your chest.
- As you're visualizing, notice the sensations or feelings arising within you. Acknowledge them, whether they're intense or subtle.
- Visualize the light within you beginning to expand and grow brighter with every deep breath you take. Keep visualizing and feeling this expansion until it feels as if this light is filling up the entire room you're sitting in.
- Once you're shining your own light as brightly as you feel you can, consider the consciousness of God. How do you imagine the grand consciousness of which you are a spark?
- Feel the light you've built becoming enveloped by a much grander light, whose power you are now calling upon.

- Allow yourself to be in reverence of the divinity that you're experiencing. Surrender to a moment of remembering what it feels like to be divinely connected in this way.
- Stay in this state for as long as you feel you can. Keep breathing, pushing all of the light outward with as much strength and intensity as you can.
- When you feel that you can't hold it any longer and the energy is dropping, visualize all of that light returning to you, to the place from which it came, and being integrated into your being, ready to be evoked or accessed at any point in time.
- Slowly bring your awareness back to your body, and when you're ready, gently open your eyes.

This is the power Da Vinci unwittingly captured – the perfect state of human and soul, unified, expanded into spiritual mastery.

The more you access this power, the more you'll realize it speaks to you. Not in words, but in energy. In sensation. In knowing. The soul has its own ancient language. And to truly harness your spiritual abilities, you must learn it.

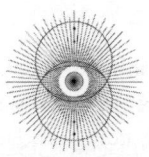

Chapter 9

LEARNING YOUR OWN LANGUAGE

Learning to interpret energetic information is like learning your own personal language. It's unique to you and entirely shaped by how your energy field interacts with your mind. No one can teach you exactly how yours works; they can only guide you toward discovering it for yourself.

But here's what you need to know to begin: Your psychic senses operate from the same place as your imagination (which is why we reawakened that to begin with).

Clairvoyance, such as psychic sight, appears in the same mental space where you would picture a yellow flower sitting in a field of green grass. Just by reading that sentence, you probably imagined it. However clearly or vaguely it appeared for you, it appeared in the place where clairvoyant impressions will show up.

And they might not ever be more vivid than that yellow flower. Sometimes clairvoyance is just a quick flash or a faint overlay in the background of your mind.

Now think of a song you know well and 'hear' it playing in your mind. That inner sound? That's where clairaudience – psychic hearing – will appear. Clairaudience doesn't show up as some booming voice from the heavens, but a *slightly heightened layer of inner awareness* that feels as if it arises from within.

It's probably not what you expected. But remember that's exactly what keeps so many people from discovering their abilities – their expectations.

Instead of waiting for something massive or profoundly mystical to hit you, begin listening out for soft nudges, little impressions.

Every time you notice one, your energetic perception expands. When you interact with energy, whether it's a person, a spirit, place, object, or even an intention, you're not just picking up information, you're actually merging with it in some way. There's a blending, a resonance. You tune your own field to that field, and new sensations, thoughts, and insights begin to arise.

Sometimes the energy you pick up feels distinctly *other*, as if something new has entered your awareness. Other times, it feels as if your own memories, emotions, or thoughts are being highlighted and something is using *your own experiences* to help guide you toward a broader understanding of the energy. This doesn't mean you're making it up. It means the energy is working with the most effective tools available, which are your own memories. This is what we call 'a frame of reference.'

But in order to identify what's coming from something or someone else, you have to first be deeply familiar with what's already your own.

Knowing Your Own Energy

You have to know the tone, feel, rhythm and make-up of your own energy. Otherwise, how will you recognize what's not yours?

This is why emotional awareness and self-inquiry are foundational. The more clearly you know yourself, the more easily you'll notice the moment something unfamiliar begins to ripple through your field.

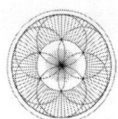

CREATING A BALL OF YOUR OWN ENERGY

This practice will help you become familiar with the feel and language of your own energy field.

Step 1: Set Your Intention

- Find a quiet space where you won't be disturbed. Allow your body to settle and your mind to soften. Put on music that feels calming, floaty, or uplifting — something that helps you feel expansive. Let your only expectation be curiosity.

Step 2: Awaken the Sensation

- Place your hands in front of you, a couple of inches apart. Gently move them toward and away from each other, as though you're pressing on an invisible cushion. Imagine your energy moving out of both hands, meeting itself between your palms. Notice what sensation arises: it may feel like magnetism, pressure, tingling, warmth, or something else entirely. However subtle, trust what you sense — your energy always communicates in your own language.

Step 3: Create and Grow the Energy

- As you feel that subtle sensation, imagine a small ball of energy forming between your hands. This is your creation, a tangible piece of your own field. Let it expand and strengthen as you move your hands. See its color, its glow. Notice how its qualities mirror your auric field and reflect aspects of your own energetic tone.

Step 4: Play and Explore

- Bounce the ball gently from hand to hand. Enlarge it to the size of a beach ball, then condense it to the size of a golf ball, noticing how the pressure shifts as you do so. Let yourself play with it. This playful state is the doorway to flow — the more you enjoy it, the stronger it becomes.

Step 5: Tune in with Your Senses

- Sight: What color is your energy ball? Does it shift or change?
- Sound: Bring it toward your ear. Imagine you can hear its vibration. What tone or rhythm does it carry?
- Feeling: Notice the weight, pressure, and movement as it interacts with your hands.

Each perception may be subtle — just a fleeting image or a faint sound in your inner awareness — but trust these impressions, no matter how slight they seem.

Step 6: Merge with Your Energy

- Place the ball gently onto your stomach and feel the energy amplify there. Experience a heightened awareness of your own energy. Then lift the ball to your crown, filling it with white light as it activates your pineal gland. Let the energy cascade down through your chakras, cleansing and balancing as it flows, before catching the ball at your feet.

Step 7: Enter the Flow State

- Let yourself play with this energy — sway, dance, or simply flow with it in your body. Notice what thoughts, emotions, or intuitive insights arise as you surrender to the rhythm. Your energy is intelligent; the more you release control and enter the flow, the more naturally it will speak to you.

Step 8: Reflect

- When you've finished, take a moment to notice how your body feels, what you saw, heard, or sensed, and what kind of impressions arose. This is your energy speaking in its own unique language.

Your energy is always communicating. It knows how to process and exchange information without your conscious input. It's your *mind* that needs refinement - the training, the practice, the quiet attunement. That's what opens the channel.

And the more emotionally regulated you are, the clearer your field becomes.

The less internal noise there is, the more easily new information can be recognized.

Interpreting the Energy Around You

When something enters your energy, whether it's the mood of a room, the intention behind someone's words, or the emotional residue left behind in a place, you feel it. Your energy responds to it in real time. You might feel a shift in your body, or you might get a flash of imagery or a wave of emotion that doesn't quite feel like yours. It's like an echo landing on the surface of your field. And once it hits, you interpret it.

Interpretation can happen in all kinds of ways. It might be felt as a gut reaction, a sudden insight, a memory surfacing, or a physical sensation that doesn't seem to fit. It may move through your senses: inner sight, inner hearing, inner knowing. Some impressions are fleeting. Others linger or keep returning until you acknowledge them.

But however it comes, a message is rarely dropped into your lap in a perfectly polished sentence. It's subtle. It appears in the *background* of your awareness.

Sometimes the information comes like a game of charades – just a gesture, a flash, a reference. Other times, it rides on the back of a memory or a familiar image. Your consciousness has to gently lean into these impressions.

But your energy is intelligent. It draws upon your own thoughts and lived experiences. It makes things easy for you through synchronicity.

Sometimes it makes things *so* easy and obvious that you question their legitimacy. You think, *But that's just me making it up*. But actually, your own energy is always communicating. It always has been, only now, you're learning how to listen.

Finding Your Flow State

After learning to access the power and beginning to recognize subtle energetic information, the next phase is to let that energy carry you. To stop trying to control the process and instead allow it to move through you – effortlessly, instinctively, naturally. This is where flow begins.

Once you've successfully evoked your power and married it with your chosen intention – once you've found that coherence – it tends to take over anyway. No matter what the energetic task at hand may be.

You don't need to worry about whether doubt is infiltrating your mind or if you're 'doing it right,' because it simply all begins to happen organically. You don't need to control or micro-manage the process. You are responsible for building your power's momentum – initiating the connection – but once it begins, you won't need to 'try' at all. It will overcome you and will simply be happening.

This is the flow state. It's a space where your inner magic can rise to the surface and move with ease and grace.

Imagine a fire dancer, twirling fire as they move. They find their rhythm, then enter a state where they're just moving and dancing – they aren't having to think about what their hands are doing. They're enchanted by the present moment.

That moment of surrender, of being overtaken by something, is what you're looking for when working with your spiritual power.

Keeping the Mind Busy

The mind often needs a task in order for that to happen – something to focus on, a doorway to open. When the dancer has the fire as their mind's focal point, their soul rises and that powerful energy is evoked within that moment.

This is a big part of why you'll often see mediums scribbling and doodling on a piece of paper during their readings – they're giving their mind something to focus on so that they can stop it from interrupting their process and allow the magic to flow.

It's also a part of why meditators focus upon their breath, a visualization, or a mantra.

The mind is the blocker of all endeavors, so in our energetic endeavors, finding a way to keep it busy allows us to better achieve what we're setting out to do. It's all about finding the tricks to keep your mind at bay and enter a deeper sense of surrender and trust.

Initiating the Process

One of the first things I teach my students is that in order to access energy or deliver a reading, you have to begin without knowing exactly where it's going to take you.

When you're wanting to tap into any kind of energy, you can't simply go into a place of stillness and wait for something to hit you. You can't wait for it to begin. You have to initiate your connection by trusting yourself and going for it. With trust and the correct energetic conditions, you'll always find yourself falling into that flow state. But you don't get there through silence and stillness, you get there by taking the first few steps and building the momentum.

The ego will always try to stop you, to try to make you feel more prepared. It wants to know where everything is going to end up and how each step of the process is going to look. It wants to ask questions. *Wait, so what am I doing again? What should happen next? Am I actually doing this right?*

You need to just push yourself over that edge, like a bungee-jump facilitator with a stubborn person who won't take the leap. A simple little nudge and you're off.

You find the flow state by releasing expectations, and simply beginning...

If you have a practice that allows you to move into a flow state by giving your mind a break and just being fully present with something, it will serve you greatly in your attempts to connect with something energetically. It'll help you connect with the creative nature of your soul energy.

Whether through a form of dance, movement, yoga, or singing and connecting with the energy of your voice, or creating art or having another kind of creative outlet, becoming familiar with getting into a state of flow is one of the most beneficial things you can ever do. No distractions, nowhere else to be, just completely present, getting into a flow – and a beautiful vibration.

One of the most powerful and accessible ways to do this is through movement. Put on headphones (or power up your speaker), play music that stirs something in you, and let yourself move, dance, stretch, flow. Or go someplace beautiful, walk to the music, and let your soul rise.

Then you're connected and being moved by that energy without even realizing how it all happened. It's an intelligence and you can't control it. Once evoked, you must allow it to take over, to do what it does best – move intelligently. It's how energy speaks.

Enjoying the Experience

When done correctly, successful energy work – whether it's spirit communication, healing, or manifestation – feels easy and effortless. If the energy feels sluggish, difficult, or challenging, the first thing you need to check is how you're feeling. If you're not enjoying the process, then you're not cultivating enough soul power for it to flow with ease.

The best readings I've ever done have also been the easiest. The greatest manifestations I've ever called in were the ones that felt fun and exciting to energize. When the energy feels good, it works with minimal effort.

And that feeling? That's your spiritual power, flowing through you in real time.

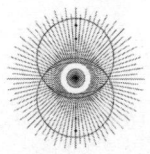

Chapter 10

ILLUMINATING THE DARKNESS

All that we perceive of this world is Source itself and that which Source has created through being here. From the pyramids and temples of the ancients to the concrete-jungle cities of today to all the art and inventions along the way; all of it has come about as a result of creative consciousness entering this playground of discovery and imagination.

A creative consciousness is a spark of the divine, creating within the world it's currently inhabiting.

As soul beings who are a creative consciousness in a physical existence, we are always creating – and not just on a physically tangible level either. We are unconsciously interacting within many realms, dimensions, and energetic spaces simply through existing. There is far more to understand when opening up to your spiritual power and abilities than just what is of 'our world' and what is of 'the spirit world.'

Energetic Imprints

Whether it be through the thoughts or emotions that we're having or the words that we're speaking, we continuously leave behind a trail of energy that's imprinted upon the environments that we move through. In all cases, the stronger the emotional response that we have to something in any particular moment, the stronger the potency of the imprint left behind.

These energetic imprints can be sensed and felt, especially by those who are sensitive to energy. Have you ever walked into a space and felt instantly uplifted or suddenly heavy, without knowing why? That's the energy left behind by others. Joy, peace, anger, grief – all of it lingers. It builds. And the more energy that's contributed to it, the stronger and more alive that imprint becomes.

Some of these imprints fade with time, while others deepen and develop, especially in places where many people have responded emotionally over long periods. Think of the energy you feel inside a temple, church, or mosque, even if you're not religious. The awe, reverence, and love of thousands of people over centuries creates a powerful energetic field within that space. That energy interacts with every new person who enters, influencing and amplifying their experience. In response, those individuals contribute more of the same energy, intensifying the field even further.

This energetic weaving is also why memorials and tragic locations often feel heavy, even if nothing traumatic physically happened there. People arrive, reflect, mourn, imagine, and have their own emotional responses, and their responses create a tangible energy that settles into the space. The collective memory becomes palpable, almost as if the air itself becomes heavier.

One of the most intense energetic imprints I've ever felt was in a beautiful castle in Belgium. From the outside, it looked inviting, surrounded by greenery and a calm moat. But the moment I stepped inside, panic, anxiety, and fear flooded my body without warning or reason. The energy in that place was overwhelming, and the only thought running through me was: *Get out*. But it was too late – there was a one-way path through the castle.

Room by room, I felt the echo of suffering, pain, and torment. It was a place where horrific torture had been performed – very frequently. I hadn't known this prior to entering.

At one point, I felt as if I'd been struck on the back of my neck – a heavy sensation that blurred my vision. Turning a corner, I saw a sign explaining the room had once been used for neck torture.

When I finally exited the building, I collapsed on the grass outside. I lay there for over an hour, trying to process what had just happened and to gather myself. I hadn't felt spirits, or that I was being haunted, I'd felt memories deeply imprinted in the space. It was as if the castle itself had remembered. And I, being wide-open energetically, had interacted with those memories. I'd responded to them, taken them in, and added to them, unconsciously feeding their potency with my own reaction.

That's the power of our energy. It doesn't just fade away, it weaves itself into the world.

Our emotional responses, whether dramatic or subtle, program the space we're in, just as we're influenced by what's already been programmed into it. And when enough people engage with an energetic imprint, especially in similar ways, it starts to behave almost as if it's alive.

These energies aren't intelligent – they only *appear* that way because of how much energy and attention has been given to them. They become so strong they mimic awareness. But really, they're just echoes repeating what's been programmed into them. They're neutral – until a creative consciousness comes along, engages with them, and gives them meaning and direction.

Looking After Your Own Energetic Space

And this is why it's so important to consciously tend to the energy in your own space. If energy builds, then your home, your room, or even your work space will begin to reflect whatever energy has been dominant there.

Emotional residue can accumulate like dust. Over time, it can influence your mood, your thoughts, even your clarity. And based upon how we react to a space after someone has had an argument in it, imagine the effect our space has after a long bout of depression or grief.

Clearing your space of negativity, heaviness, or stagnant emotion is good spiritual hygiene. It's one of the most important things to do to find your way out of those heavy times we all encounter in our lives. When we invite in high, beautiful frequencies and intentionally infuse our space with peace, joy, and love, we start to feel differently immediately.

When you understand that your energy is constantly weaving into the world, you become empowered.

You get to decide how you respond to energy, how you engage with it, and what kind of energy you're contributing to. You can uplift a space through the sheer power of your presence. It's not the crystals, white sage or palo santo in your hand that clears the heaviness, but *you*, the creative consciousness holding them! It's your awareness, your intention, and your energy that have the power to clear, bless, or transform a space.

When you've been through a challenging month, week, day, or even just a heavy hour and you feel that the energy around you is thick, stagnant, or simply *off*, this exercise is a powerful way to begin shifting it.

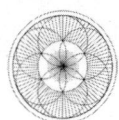

CLEARING YOUR SPACE

Clearing your space energetically can support your energy, relieve you of unwanted repetitive patterns, and open you back up to soul-aligned flow. Here's how:

Step 1. Choose Your Instrument

Start by selecting a cleansing tool that feels good to you. This could be:

- a sage stick or palo santo
- a singing bowl, drum, or any musical instrument
- a crystal you love to work with
- vibrationally attuned music playing through a speaker
- your own hands clapping or simply your voice

It doesn't matter what you choose. What matters is your intention. It's your creative power that clears the energy, not the tool. The tool simply becomes an extension of your intention.

Step 2. Sense the Space

- Begin walking slowly through your space. Let your awareness guide you. Tune into each room, each area, each corner. Energy tends to gather in the corners of ceilings and tucked-away places, just like cobwebs. Run your hand through the air around these areas, particularly the upper corners, and notice what you sense. Do certain spaces feel heavier, colder, or denser? Do you feel pulled, contracted, or emotionally off in specific areas?

- You don't need to know what the energy is, where it came from, or what it means. As your intuitive perception develops, those insights may come, but right now, just feel.

Step 3. Clear Intuitively

Once you've sensed where energy needs to move from, you can begin clearing it.

- Light your sage or palo santo, press 'play' on the music, or begin playing your instrument. Clap your hands. Sing. Let your movements be guided by instinct.

- Move slowly and consciously, visualizing the smoke or sound vibrating through the room. Imagine it lifting, unraveling, and transmuting dense energy as it moves. You might see the heavy energy turning into light, dissolving into particles, or simply being carried away.

Believe that it is clearing and it will be.

- Move through the entire space, room by room. Some rooms may require more time. Trust your intuition.

Step 4. Invite in Beauty

Once the space has been cleared, the next step is to fill it — to consciously invite a beautiful, soulful, and enriching energy into your space.

- Evoke your soul power. Feel joy. Feel gratitude. Feel a sense of elevation and allow that inner light to rise to the surface.

- Visualize your energy expanding outward, infusing the space with beautiful colors, maybe golden light, crystalline hues, pinks, or blues — whatever feels right to you in the moment. See this light bathing the walls, floors, and ceilings, encoding them with frequencies of peace, joy, love, and deep support.

- Feel the shift. The brightness. The life returning to the space.

Step 5. Seal with Joy (Optional but Powerful)

- If you feel called to do so, play your favorite music — something that lifts your spirits — and dance! Sing. Laugh. Have fun. Let your energy be light, playful, and alive. Infuse the space with joy. This frequency leaves one of the most powerful energetic imprints of all.

Once you've completed this process, pause.

Notice how different the space feels. Notice how you feel.

You've just shifted an entire field of energy — and opened space for more beautiful, expansive, and soul-aligned frequencies to enter.

See how miraculously everything can change, and enjoy the results!

Understanding Ghosts and Entities

On the subject of energy, there are few topics in spirituality that generate more confusion and unnecessary fear than ghosts and dark energies or 'entities.' I'm talking about entities in the common sense of a malicious spirit out to siphon your life-force. It's a topic that many don't realize they're wasting so much of their power on. But when clearly understood, these very topics become a powerful opportunity to release fear, deepen into soul embodiment, and step further into spiritual authority.

Let's begin by stating this clearly: Ghosts and entities aren't conscious spirits with malicious intent. They are energetic imprints left behind from unresolved trauma and emotion.

They are lacking in self-awareness, but often gain energy through human fear, fascination, and belief.

Do You Need Protection?

There is no energetic force that ever has more power or more influence over your energy than you do.

No energy can override the embodied beliefs of a being that creative consciousness runs through. You are a spark of the

Infinite, a living conduit of divine light. What could possibly overpower that?

The only thing darkness cannot coexist with is the light. And the moment you stand in yours, anything that's not of that vibration cannot energetically remain within it.

You are not vulnerable to things like ghosts or entities. You are a soul, born of the same light that created the entire omniverse. And when you remember that, there's no energy that can touch you without invitation or consent.

As always, it all comes back down to the beliefs you embody.

Everything that's ever affected you energetically has only done so because it's been, on some level, welcomed or engaged with. Not consciously, but through your belief, fear, or energetic agreement. The most common way people unknowingly open themselves to lower energies like this is, ironically, by believing they need protection from them in the first place.

When people feel the need to protect themselves from spirits, entities, or negative energies, they are unknowingly giving their power away and making themselves susceptible to the very thing they're trying to avoid. Protection is a practice rooted in fear, insecurity, and distrust – therefore protection rituals only reinforce each of those things. Fear attracts more fear. Believing you're vulnerable makes you vulnerable. Not because you are, but because your consciousness is creative and you've just used yours to open a doorway to the very interaction you were trying to avoid.

Fear and distrust are not conducive approaches to soul embodiment. They distance you from the intelligence that moves through you.

The only protection you ever truly need is a deep, embodied knowing of who you are and how powerful you are. That alone creates an energetic field that is sovereign, free from external influence, and entirely in command of itself.

The truth is, the most powerful protection you can ever have is knowing you don't need any at all.

Energetic Residues

Many people ask whether ghosts are real, or whether spirits can become trapped between dimensions. The answer is not as black and white as many would like it to be, but the short version is this: Yes, ghosts are real, but they're not what they're commonly perceived to be. As already mentioned, ghosts are energetic imprints left behind from intense emotion or unresolved trauma, the parts of a life that are too dense to be carried into the high frequency of the spirit world.

But there's so much more to understand about the realms of energy than just our world and the spirit world. And a ghost, interestingly enough, actually has nothing to do with the spirit world at all.

When a person dies, their consciousness – their true self – immediately returns to the soul state. There is no 'deciding' whether to 'go into the light' or not. There's no limbo, no halfway space where the spirit can get stuck. That's a human projection built on a misunderstanding of how divine energy moves and flows.

Spirit is divine light. You cannot 'go into' something that you already are.

The soul, in its original form, is light – and light cannot linger in lower-vibrational density once it has released the body. A soul needs a physical form in order to experience itself within lower realms. Once the body is released, it returns to its original, non-physical state. This is the part of us that is eternal consciousness – the rest of our energy is temporary.

But energy cannot be created or destroyed, it can only be transformed. So when a person dies, their body returns to the earth, their soul returns to Spirit, and what's left... remains – dispersing itself into the energetic tapestry of the space.

This is simply energetic residue – the layers of a life that were never realized or resolved. The same goes for imprints from experiences that carried an immense emotional charge. If a person dies a traumatic death, experiencing intense fear, pain, or anger, the energy of that moment can be so strong that it stamps itself onto the energetic fabric of that environment, leaving a trace of its own. These impressions don't have self-awareness. They aren't conscious. But they can feel that way to those who come across them.

This is where the concept of 'ghosts' or 'earthbound spirits' comes in. What people interpret as a trapped soul is more accurately a piece of a soul that was too heavy to ascend with them when their body died. It's leftover information that lingers near the Earth plane, energy that is programmed to echo the heavy memories of that life on a loop.

These energetic imprints could be compared to artificial intelligence. They seem intelligent – they engage and interact with us in a certain way – but only because they've been programmed to do so. Not because there is a conscious force driving them.

Much like the castle I visited in Belgium, these residues can feel vivid, thick, even sentient when engaged with. But they're nothing to be fearful of – there's no sinister force trying to defend its space or tormented soul who's refusing to leave. They're echoes of an earthly experience, still intertwined with the walls, the floor, or the surrounding field.

Back in the Game

You know how earlier, when talking about reincarnation (in Chapter 5), I mentioned that we re-enter the game at the level we last left it? Well, the way this works is that many of those imprints, residual energies, or unresolved frequencies that we left behind in our last 'death' return to us in our subsequent birth. They tie in with our soul contracts. They are our karma. But Spirit doesn't see this as punishment. It sees it as the learning continuing.

These things can't be worked through in the spirit world, so we begin again by taking them on in the next life. There's no homework in heaven, obviously.

Understanding Leads to Power

There's no denying that these residual energies can be felt. In fact, lower-vibrational energies are much easier to sense and interact with than actual spiritual beings. They vibrate at a frequency far closer to our own than the spirit world does.

Because they've been created from earthly experiences, they remain tethered to the earthly realm. That's why people tend to sense 'a haunting' more easily than they experience direct communication with Spirit. To connect with the spirit world, a vibrational shift is required, but these energies can be perceived almost effortlessly. Because of this, interactions with them can feel incredibly tangible, visceral, and often quite confronting or scary.

But remember these energies don't have self-awareness. They aren't 'out to get you.' They're simply moving with the momentum they've been given.

When a creative consciousness encounters them, it responds in a way that either amplifies or dissolves them, based on the frequency and level of understanding it brings to the interaction.

The moment you *believe* something is demonic or malicious, your reaction feeds that illusion. As creative consciousnesses, we must remember:

Whatever we give energy to, we give life to.

That's why understanding is so powerful. To understand what these energies actually are is to reclaim your power.

These energetic residues are why many people fear opening up to the spirit world, but once you know what they are, the next time you come across one, it simply won't affect you. Trust me, you'll find it more difficult to get a piece of gum off your shoe than to get rid of an 'entity' or stop yourself interacting with a 'ghost.'

Soul 'Rescue'

When a medium believes they are communicating with a lost soul and sending it into the light, they aren't guiding a trapped spirit – the soul is already in the light. What they're doing is helping to transmute the energy that soul left behind. In fact, the light they think they're sending that 'soul' to *is* the soul itself.

The medium, through spiritual connection, is actually calling the soul's essence into contact with what was left behind, creating a field where those 'unfinished' frequencies can be resolved. That process is real, but it's not a rescue. It's more like a service. It's an opportunity for that soul to clean up what it has left behind. And it works because the medium has chosen to meet the energy with a helpful intention.

Spiritual Authority

Which brings us to the most important point: You always get to decide what you interact with, and how.

When you decide, with clarity, that you're only available for what you allow and invite, everything outside of that cannot exist in your field. It has no power without your agreement.

There is no force in this universe that can override the will of a being who remembers their soul. There's nothing more powerful than the light that created all of existence. That is the true nature of spiritual authority.

You aren't here to fear anything – you're here to remember that you create everything.

So, when it comes to protection, the real question is: Do you believe you need it?

If your answer is 'yes,' then you will. That belief will give power to exterior influences and you'll need the prayers, rituals, and visualization techniques to manage them.

If your answer is 'no,' if you trust in the light that you are, then nothing has energetic access to you. There will be no space in your field for interference.

This isn't about denial or pretending dark energies don't exist. It's about understanding what they *are*, and that they don't have any power over you. You can clear them, disconnect from them, and override them just by remembering your true nature. You aren't subject to anything in this world unless you believe you are.

You can't be an empowered conduit of the spirit world while worrying about accidentally connecting with something dangerous. Fear and hesitation weaken your soul connection.

When you remember your power, nothing uninvited can remain in your presence.

You don't have to fight darkness, you only have to stand in your light.

So, when fear arises, don't contract. Don't defend. Expand. And remember who and what you are: divine universal energy.

With infinite potential.

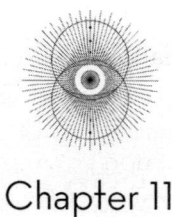

Chapter 11

DISCOVERING YOUR INFINITE POTENTIAL

In the development of my trance mediumship, I built a very close connection with my guide Lazarus. One night, I entered the altered state and surrendered to his presence. My sister was sitting with me, hoping to speak with him. We were out the back of the house, in a small workshop I'd converted into a humble reading space. The roof was made of thin, transparent plastic, and on that night torrential rain was pouring down with full force, pounding loudly above us.

I could feel Lazarus's presence building, but I couldn't fully surrender to him because the sound was so intense. Still, I persisted. I kept inviting him closer.

Then, in this deep semi-present state, I heard words come out of my mouth: 'We need to stop the rain. He is too distracted.'

I had no idea I was about to say that. But within moments, the thick clouds parted. The rain stopped. Like magic.

My awareness sank, and in that same moment, Lazarus stepped forward fully and said with a smile, 'That's better.'

After sharing guidance and insights, his presence began to fade, and as I opened my eyes and the séance came to a close, the rain once again came bucketing down. It was as though a gap had been carved in the sky just for the time he needed to speak.

That was the night I learned it was within the power of a soul to control the elements.

But that wasn't a miraculous discovery. It's something ancient cultures have known for centuries.

The Hawaiian rain dancers of Waimea continue the practices of their ancestors as guardians of their land. They have been known to summon rain, wind, and sunshine – whatever the land is in need of – and they do it with a remarkably high rate of success. And they are only one of many incredible examples.

Today, many people assume we are more advanced than those who came before. But when you look at what they were capable of – what they built, what they knew, and what they achieved – perhaps it's not that they were less advanced, but that they were tuned into a level of consciousness we've long since forgotten.

That display of power from Lazarus isn't the only time I've seen Spirit bend the elements. I've seen faces in the clouds that look unmistakably like the loved one someone was calling to. I've watched spirits move objects, make lights flicker, switch on radios, and change the temperature in a room – all without a body. Just energy.

I remember when my dad once asked his own father, Roger, or 'Roge,' as he was often known, to send him a sign. Soon after, my dad had to reset a password on an important business account. The new one would be automatically generated. It could've been anything.

When the email came through, the new password was: Roge07. His father's name and the year of his passing. Perfectly sequenced. Undeniable.

How can a being without a body do these things?

But the real question is: If they can, why can't we?

The truth is: *We can.*

Our Miraculous Powers

The more time I've spent working with the spirit world, the more I've come to understand something extraordinary: all the miracles they're capable of are ultimately within *us* too. The intelligence they operate through is the same force that exists within our own souls. It isn't something we only acquire through death – it resides within us all right now.

We've been led to believe that the miraculous is of the spirit world, and of angelic or godly forces. And we've been led to believe that that's not what we are – but it's *exactly* what we are.

> When we access our power, when we embody it, what unfolds can be nothing short of miraculous.

Shifting Our Attention

The reason souls become capable of miraculous occurrences after shedding their physical bodies isn't because they suddenly gain more power. They simply shed the filter.

When we're incarnated, our attention is grounded in our human experience. We learn to navigate reality through what we can see, touch, and measure. The very moment we release the body, our consciousness expands – massively. We remember that we weren't just here during that incarnation, we were everywhere else at once too. And in that state of expanded awareness, remembering who and what we truly are, manipulating energy and bending reality to our will isn't supernatural at all. It's simply natural.

This is the key: To access this miraculous power of our soul while incarnated, we must shift our awareness further back toward our soul self, the part of us that still exists within the spirit world.

What I have learned through my trance-mediumship development and exploration is that profound miracles happen when the presence of Spirit is strong and the human, analytical, and logical mind is surrendered. It happens only through experiencing yourself as the divine force that you are. When you can find ways to shift your focus and perceive yourself as that, its power will run through you. But you have to be able to take enough focus away from your mind and body in order for that to happen.

Meditation

That's where meditation ultimately becomes a powerful tool of transformation. And before you roll your eyes at me, just hear me out on this one. Meditation isn't simply about finding inner peace and tranquility, it's about becoming aware of your mind's habits and training it to not interrupt your focus.

People so often say that they 'can't meditate' because their mind wanders, but becoming aware of the wandering mind is the exact point and purpose of meditation in the first place.

> *'The quieter you become, the more you can hear.'*
> RAM DASS

The ego is a master of deception and distraction. Upon your attempts to quieten your mind, it feeds you thoughts that are intended to sabotage that very stillness. It jumps from topic to topic, reminds you of all the other more important things that you should be doing with your time, and leads you to fixate upon things that will be likely to distract you and make you give up.

If that happens for you, it doesn't mean that *you can't meditate*. That's actually how it starts for everyone.

The art of meditation – of quieting this so-called 'monkey mind' – is a process of continuously being interrupted and then returning to your intended focus, which is stillness. Over and over again, your attention is pulled away, yet each time you bring it back, you're gaining more power and control over your ego and its influence over you. You're retraining it, stopping it from interrupting you, distracting you, and stealing your focus (and your peace and tranquility).

I dare you to sit in silence for five minutes, to just breathe and attempt to find stillness in your mind. It will give you an idea of how much control this part of your mind currently has over you – and it might just shock you to find out!

That monkey mind is what brings you back to your physicality, back to your mental space, over and over again. It's what takes your focal point away from your soul self and distances you from your innate power.

Nurturing Our Soul Self

The only way that we can find our soul self is by allowing stillness into our physical and mental selves. It requires a balance of all aspects of the self to reach our own greatness. However, nurturing the soul self is something that the vast majority of the world's population have been missing – and it's this aspect that has been nurtured by people seen to have gained some kind of extraordinary abilities or mystical superpowers. Monks in Tibet and shamans in Africa have developed their energetic power enough to achieve and demonstrate levitation, for example, and others have used their telekinetic abilities to move objects with their minds.

The power that we obtain when we return to our original state is tremendous. Those in that discarnate space often use it to reach back into our world to give us incredible messages and signs that they're still with us. But for those of us who are in the incarnate world, this power can have many more uses that are of great service to us.

Because, as fascinating as it may be, making lights flicker with energy alone serves little practical purpose – beyond proving that it can be done. Instead, we can use this power to completely transform our lives, shape our reality, become conduits of higher frequencies, and magnetize to us the experiences we desire to have in this incarnation. We can become aligned with our highest and most fulfilled selves.

In the UK, trained groups of children have developed their third-eye vision and extra-sensory-perception to the point where they can read books and navigate obstacle courses while blindfolded.[4]

In India, spiritual gurus radiate such an immense energy field that people report profound activations simply by being in their presence. Energy healers across the world have been known to shift mental and physical illnesses where modern medicine has failed. Shamans of South America become one with the Mother Earth and navigate the dimensions between. Mediums bridge worlds and psychics interpret energy, guiding others through the intelligence of their own higher consciousness. And on top of that, thousands are learning to harness their soul's power to simply live attuned, guided, and abundant lives.

These are all manifestations of the soul's power.

**The more we align with our true nature,
the more reality bends to our will.**

---

[4] Earing, R., 'Super Learning' program for ages 5–12, ICU Academy: www.live4energy.co.uk/icu-academy [Accessed 15 September 2025]

When we remember who and what we truly are, and experience ourselves as this, the world becomes a playground of limitless potential. That is the kind of existence that your soul came here hoping to experience.

And that is the journey you're on now: to remember who and what you truly are – and to live from that truth. To create miracles.

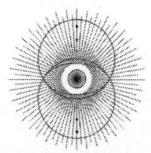

Chapter 12

THE ALCHEMY OF BELIEF: HOW MIRACLES BECOME REALITY

Whether you realize it or not, you're already shaping your experience of reality. Your energetic field is always responding to your thoughts, emotions, and beliefs. The key is to become conscious of this process and learn to direct it with mindful intention.

Your energetic field is like an intelligent supercomputer, and you are its operator. It does exactly what it's told, responding instantly to the instructions of both your conscious and subconscious minds. Your conscious mind holds your wishes and intentions, while your subconscious governs your expectations and deeply held beliefs, and controls 95 percent of your thoughts. This makes beliefs far more powerful than fleeting conscious intentions.

The Power of Belief

You are the most powerful creator of your own reality, and understanding the power of belief helps you to see how and why.

For an intention to shape your energetic state, it has to become a belief. Only then does it ripple through your conscious and subconscious minds, and become reality.

While physical manifestations in the material world take time, energetic shifts happen instantly:

+ If you believe your energy is being drained by something, it will drain. You will feel flat and tired.

+ If you believe your field is filling up with beautiful, high-vibrational energy, you will start to experience its uplifting effect.

+ If you believe others can curse you, put a hex on you, or affect your energy with their negative intentions, they will be able to do so.

+ If you believe you have complete power over your own energy and that no one else can influence it without your permission, then that will be your reality too.

Consciously Choosing Your Beliefs

Since beliefs shape your reality no matter what they are, you can see how crucial it is to align yourself with ones that empower you and expand your potential.

Before accepting a belief, decide whether it will help you create the reality you want. If it won't serve you or lead you anywhere positive, that's a good sign to toss it aside and decide that it won't be true for you. You govern it all.

You always get to decide what you are aligning yourself with energetically.

Most people just do it unconsciously, but through the remembrance of your true self and true power, you will never have to go back to doing that.

The Strength of Imagination

Studies and scans have shown that the same areas of the brain are activated whether a person is imagining something or actually experiencing it.[5]

This means your brain doesn't entirely differentiate between what is real and what it's told is real. As the director of your own energetic field, you can use that to your advantage to create whatever energetic reality you choose.

This is why, when performing any energetic practice, you must send the signal to your brain that it's already happening. Through your brain's direct connection to your energetic field, it becomes your reality. If the belief is fully embodied, without hesitation or doubt, the energetic shift happens instantly.

---

5   Ganis, G., *et al.* (2004), 'Brain Areas Underlying Visual Mental Imagery and Visual Perception: An fMRI Study', *Cognitive Brain Research*, 20(2), July: 226–41.

The way to send that signal, as those studies have revealed, is through your imagination. This is exactly why visualization is a thread found in almost every spiritual practice, and in many religious ones too.

> **Visualization is the fastest gateway to transforming your energetic state and aligning yourself with your desired intention.**

For example, during meditation, when you visualize a white beam of light entering through the crown of your head, while *genuinely believing* it's happening, high-vibrational energy *does* begin moving through that exact space. Your intelligent supercomputer responds to the command it's given. Every time!

The only thing that interrupts this process is doubt. If the ego interjects with, *This is silly* or *I'm making this up*, it weakens the effect. But if belief is strong, the energy will move as per instruction.

Engaging the Senses

And imagination isn't just about what you *see* internally. Often, when you begin to imagine something happening, it naturally begins to evoke something from within you. So, the feeling follows.

When you acknowledge that feeling, it further affirms to your brain that the experience is real. The more visceral your imagination, the more powerfully your brain registers it as real – and therefore the stronger your energetic response to it is.

That's why, on top of visualizing your intention, you should try to engage as many senses as possible:

- ✦ What would it feel like? Internally and externally?
- ✦ What sounds would accompany it?
- ✦ Would there be a scent, taste, or texture associated with it?

No matter how subtle or strong they may be, the sensations you're experiencing further reinforce to your brain that the experience is real.

If you ignore or dismiss these sensations, your subconscious will doubt the experience and limiting beliefs will take over, weakening your intention and diminishing the likelihood of bringing it into reality.

Embodying Beliefs

Remember, the power of belief is what directs your energy. This is how you create the energetic environments and settings that support your spiritual endeavors. This is the hack that leads to the most miraculous outcomes.

Embody a belief, and your energy will follow. This is how you can transform your reality from the inside out.

Tapping into your spiritual power and potential can be compared to learning to ride a bike. At first, it's just an idea. You watch others do it with ease, you listen to how it works, you imagine what it might feel like. But watching others or hearing how they do it isn't what gets you there. The only thing that ever does is actually getting on the bike.

The number one thing that stops someone from riding a bike is the belief that they can't. That belief becomes their experience. They get on, feel shaky, wobbly, and uncertain, then hesitate and tell themselves, *It's not working*. And because of that, it doesn't. But the moment they surrender the doubt and start pedaling with trust, they discover how easy and natural it really is.

It's by challenging their limiting beliefs and expanding what they previously thought was possible that they make that breakthrough. And after those first few seconds of steady balance... suddenly, they're off!

Belief and expectation are everything. What we believe we're capable of defines what we experience. And when it comes to our spiritual connection, this truth is instant. Our level of achievement, success, and capability is always a direct reflection of our self-belief.

Many people begin this path thinking they don't have 'the gift.' But that belief is the very block that is stopping them from reaching their potential.

For example, if you believe that you cannot communicate with Spirit, you will shut yourself off from the possibility of ever receiving communications from the spirit world. That's why people who are atheist through and through will never receive a sign from their loved ones in Spirit – they have created a version of reality for themselves where it isn't possible.

Our beliefs are locked within us through the neural pathways that have been formed within our brain. Those pathways determine the experience we have because they are what our perception of reality is filtered through. So, in order to change the way we see things and experience things, we literally have to break up those neural pathways and create new ones. The limitations we've embodied must be shattered so new paradigms can take form – ones where anything can become possible for us.

One of the fastest ways to do this is by seeking mystical experiences.

Doorways to Spiritual Power

Most people think mystical experiences happen after our spiritual abilities awaken – and they do. But they're also doorways to our spiritual power. They're the catalysts that shatter our expectations and dissolve our limiting beliefs. They offer the evidence the ego needs to truly accept new realms of potential. Every miraculous encounter leaves a mark on our awareness, expanding how we see reality and how we experience ourselves within it.

> *'Mystical experience is simply the realization of the soul's own nature.'*
> ALAN WATTS

As you've already seen with near-death experiences, these kinds of encounters can radically shift our perception of reality. All that soul energy that experiencers have just been reminded of starts being reflected back out into their energetic field. Coming face to face with divine truth changes everything about the way they experience themselves and the world around them.

But don't worry, you don't have to face death to have a transformative mystical experience. Whether they're subtle and common, or profound but rare, they offer the same potential: a visceral encounter with divinity that the ego can't rationalize or deny. And in that moment, your relationship with reality changes.

That's how most people miss all the magic that is possible in this world – they've accepted the reality that they've been given.

Questioning isn't the enemy of belief, it's what keeps it alive and evolving.

And yet, questioning isn't enough for the ego – it demands proof. And without that proof, it struggles to surrender and accept. But when a person shifts from skepticism into cynicism, the line between them and the miraculous becomes almost unmovable.

A cynic could witness all the evidence in the world and still reject it. And because of that, their reality would never change.

The ego is what clings to beliefs about what's possible and what's not, and until it's given a reason to change them, it remains as the barrier between us and the fullest expression of our spiritual power.

But where the ego is grounded within its rigidness, there is one thing that's powerful enough to overcome its ways in even small amounts. It's the one thing a cynic lacks: optimism.

Initiating Possibilities

In order to experience a profound relationship with your higher self, you have to be willing to accept that something better is possible. You have to be willing to dissolve old paradigms and step beyond the limits of your current understanding. You have to be willing to be proven wrong.

Think of it as a process: You experience something new, your belief changes, disrupting old neural pathways and forming new ones. Your shift of perspective shifts your energy. The realm of potential you operate within expands. Your experience of reality changes. What once seemed impossible to you becomes entirely possible, even normal. The cycle repeats as you reach toward greater potentials once again.

This is why seeking opportunities that bridge the gap between belief and knowing is essential. Once you see something, you cannot unsee it. Once you know something, you cannot unknow it.

Near-death experiencers demonstrate to us that simply witnessing something undeniable firsthand can awaken your spiritual power – instantly. And that's exactly what happened to me.

✦ ✦ ✦

When I began exploring the spirit world, I encountered things that defied all logic – things I'd never have believed, had I not seen them with my own eyes. From spirits materializing in front of me to levitating tables and physical human transfiguration, I saw what I had previously thought was impossible, and it changed everything for me from that point on.

I was 19 when I attended my first mediumship seminar – the one with Tony Stockwell that my grandfather had guided me to during my out-of-body experience. I found myself surrounded by some of the most renowned and respected mediums in the field. That week, I was introduced to spirit phenomena that shattered every belief I had about the limitations of this world.

One evening during that seminar, we attempted an age-old practice called 'table tipping.' This form of spirit communication dates back to the origins of modern spiritualism in the 1800s. It's a practice where a group of mediums surround a wooden table, place their fingertips lightly on top of it, elevate their energy, and invite the spirit world to interact with it. The idea is that through the combined energy of the group, the vibrations rise high enough for the spirits who have gathered to move the table in ways that defy physical and logical explanation.

I was equal parts eager and skeptical going into that evening. I'd always thought that mediumship was a communication of minds only, and a part of me believed that objects moving without touch was a bit far-fetched. But I was hoping to be proven wrong.

My fellow students and I were full of excited and nervous energy as we entered the room. We positioned ourselves in small groups around several tables, fingertips resting lightly on them, opening ourselves up to Spirit as directed. We spoke out loud, inviting spirits to join us and asking them to move the table.

The minutes passed and nothing happened. Doubt started creeping in and my focus was wavering when suddenly I heard cheers erupting from across the room. One of the advanced groups of mediums had experienced the first breakthrough. I turned to see their table rising, tilting, and balancing on two legs as if it had a will of its own.

My jaw dropped. There was no logical way that table could be moving in the way that it was, with only their fingertips resting on top of it.

In that moment, our hope as a group reignited. We gathered every ounce of energy and determination, and channeled it into the table in front of us, reopening ourselves to the possibility of movement. And then the wood beneath my fingertips felt as though it was coming to life, vibrating subtly, almost as if it was breathing and bending. Then soft creaks and clicks emerged from within the table. We could all sense something was about to happen. We spoke words of encouragement, thanking the spirits and urging them to move the table. And then, in an instant, it lifted, pushing upward against my fingertips.

That table didn't just lift, it moved as though it was dancing with us. It swayed from side to side, balanced on one leg and pivoted like a ballerina, then spun round so fast we had to run to keep up with it. It moved with intelligence, avoiding obstacles, changing direction.

To be absolutely sure that there was no unconscious interference, at one point we each lifted nine of our fingers, leaving just one fingertip resting lightly on the table. And to our amazement, it still moved. It was miraculous.

As the session continued, we sensed different spirits joining us, each taking turns at moving the table. Their personalities shone through in the way that it swayed and spun playfully, or gently and tenderly leaned toward a particular person as if it was embracing them. We asked questions, and the table responded with clear, intentional movements to answer them. In that moment, the laws of physics were bending to the will of Spirit.

This experience revealed to me that the spirit world's power was far beyond what I'd originally thought. Yet even after seeing the table move with my own eyes, I was still to grasp the full depth of Spirit's ability to merge with and influence the physical world.

In the days that followed, I also encountered trance mediumship for the first time. What I saw one night was beyond anything I'd imagined. Tony's persona completely shifted as a spirit blended with him. But more astonishing was the visible physical change. He seemed to become more like the spirits he was channeling, in all ways. His face morphed so much so that he became almost entirely unrecognizable at times, something that was confirmed by an entire roomful of people seeing the same thing.

When channeling the spirit of a child, Tony raised his hands to show that one hand had become childlike – very small, thin, and fragile – while the other, right next to it, remained the hand of an adult male. The room was full of bewildered people checking with the person next to them to ensure that they weren't going crazy. But this wasn't an optical illusion, this was a man's physical body changing in impossible ways, right in front of our eyes.

Throughout that demonstration of trance mediumship, other physical phenomena occurred around us too. Flashes of light and color appeared in different corners of the room, an old CD player switched itself on and off, and dramatic shifts in temperature were felt by everyone. Many even described the sensation of a physical touch on their shoulder, arm, or head.

The energy in the space was thick, potent, and tangible. What happened that night was true, undeniable magic. It felt like a crazy dream when I woke up the next morning, but I knew that for the second time in one week, what I had once believed impossible had become not only possible but unmistakably real.

Witnessing those profound phenomena for the first time activated something within me. It left me in no doubt that anything was possible, and with that certainty came an expansion of my own potential. The limited realm of belief I'd operated within was shattered. The part of my mind that had clung to the laws of physics as I understood them was blown wide open – and the result was extraordinary.

That grand shift in perspective led to a grand shift in experience.

Soon after, spirit phenomena began appearing everywhere I went. Lights flickered. Street lamps switched themselves off as I walked beneath them. Objects flew from my cabinet in the night. Books launched themselves off shelves. It felt as if I had unlocked a superpower – like Matilda discovering her telekinetic abilities.

Others noticed it too. One day, while viewing a venue for a mediumship event, I arrived before the property manager. As I approached the locked doors, they suddenly swung open. Expecting to see someone inside, I found the space completely empty. No wind, no explanation – just Spirit, clearly giving me a warm welcome.

When the property manager arrived, he was stunned. He told me the doors had been safety locked and couldn't be opened without his key. And yet I'd just watched them unlock and open themselves. I laughed and said, 'Spooky things do happen around mediums!' But I wasn't really joking.

Experiences like this became my new normal. At a dinner gathering with fellow mediums, we were deep in conversation about physical spirit phenomena when I excused myself to the restroom. As I entered, the hand dryer across the room came on by itself. I checked, and no one was there. Amused, I silently said, 'Spirit, if that was you, do it again.' A moment later, a push-tap turned itself on and released water for a few seconds.

These vivid mystical experiences reminded me of the power of Spirit – and naturally that meant I was embodying more of my own power too. That change rippled into every area of my life. I was manifesting incredible opportunities, perceiving the spirit world more clearly than ever, and simply existing in a higher emotional state.

Every profound meditation helped, every connection with the spirit world helped, every soul-nourishing moment connected me more strongly. But nothing seemed to transform my perception of reality more rapidly than encountering these physical, undeniable moments of awe.

✦ ✦ ✦

Although these are some of my favorite stories, I'm not sharing them for the spectacle. I'm sharing them because within them lies one of the greatest keys to unlocking your own divine potential: Your experience of reality is based on what you believe is possible.

Mystical experiences are moments of revelation that dissolve the old limits we place on ourselves and our reality. They stretch the boundaries of what we believe is true and open us to more of the magic of who we are.

Every time you experience something that defies what you thought was possible, your perception of reality shifts. Whether it's witnessing something miraculous performed by another person or something that is evoked from within yourself, every time you discover more of what's available to you in this world, you expand. Bit by bit, things you never thought were possible can become your new normal.

Mystical experiences can come in many ways – by stepping into a sacred site, doing deep meditation, breathwork, through plant medicine, sessions with powerful healers or mediums, past-life regressions, near-death or out-of-body experiences – but any moment that leaves you in awe, activates your energy, or expands your consciousness can show you your divine multidimensional nature and have a lasting transformational impact on you.

Naturally, the more profound the experience, the greater its impact. Near-death experiences may offer the most undeniable proof to the ego by stripping away physical identity, but consistent exposure to less extreme mystical moments can also dissolve the ego's barriers over time, and rewire your brain and therefore your perception.

When you're ready to begin harnessing your true spiritual power, my best advice is this: Step into the unknown. Be curious. Seek out experiences that challenge your beliefs about what's possible. You never know what magic is waiting for you there.

While the teachings and exercises in this book are designed to trigger mystical experiences when alone, here are some ways to begin inviting more of them into your life:

- Start a meditation practice.
- Attend a breathwork workshop.
- Book a sound-healing session.
- Meet with a healer, shaman, psychic, or medium.
- Visit a sacred location.
- Take a class in one of the spiritual arts.
- Attend a spiritual retreat.

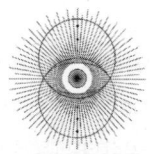

Chapter 13

SPIRIT-LED MANIFESTING: WEAVING YOUR SOUL'S DESTINY

Have you ever had one of those strange days where the same person or image keeps appearing everywhere you go? Maybe you notice someone at your first stop of the day, then see them again hours later in a completely unrelated place. It feels eerie. Random. Bizarre. But beneath the surface, there's something very real at play. It's called quantum entanglement.

We're All Connected

Quantum entanglement an amazing phenomenon that quantum physicists began sharing with the world in 1935. It's the science that shows how everything in all of existence is able to be interconnected.

Through this interconnectedness, you can unknowingly become energetically entangled with someone or something, sometimes just by placing your focus on them.

Here's how it works: When scientists take a single particle, like a photon, and split it in two, those smaller particles become *entangled*. This means they share a quantum state, even when they're far apart. And what's incredible is if you affect one of those particles in any way (like changing its spin), the other particle instantly responds, no matter how far away it is, even if it's on the other side of the world. There's no signal traveling between them and no delay. It's as if distance doesn't even exist at that level. Einstein called it 'spooky action at a distance,' because it defied everything classical physics assumed about space and time.

Now, when you zoom out from the science and look at this spiritually, it starts to make a lot of sense. When you become energetically entangled with something or someone, whether through time spent together, thought, intention, or emotion, it can start showing up both your internal and external worlds. It's like the universe is echoing the thoughts you're having. You see the same person again and again. You hear the same song everywhere you go. You notice the same animal, sign, or number pattern popping up all over the place.

This might seem like a coincidence, but it's evidence of what you're entangled with vibrationally – what you're resonating with, psychically attuned to, magnetizing, and manifesting.

When you're energetically in sync with something, whether it's a future version of yourself, a desire, a soul connection, or even a thought pattern, it starts to show up in your reality because you're already connected to it. Time and space are just the illusion that separates the unmanifest from the manifest. Therefore, to become a powerful manifestor, you must collapse time and space. Or at least your idea of them.

Powerful manifestation comes from presence and soul power. It comes through assuming and operating as if what you're aligning yourself with is already with you in the now.

Are You Psychic? Or Did You Manifest It?

What if I told you that psychically predicting something and manifesting it were actually the same thing?

For generations, psychics have been seen through a spooky, superstitious lens, often as an elderly woman in a turban with a crystal ball and hoop earrings. We've also been associated with delivering a message of doom that seals someone's fate.

But psychics aren't fortune-tellers. We don't see the future. We don't deliver certainty, because there's no such thing as a definite future reality.

What we've learned to perceive and connect to are the realms of potential. You may have already heard the term 'potential timelines' – this is the same concept.

Timelines

Psychics can connect to all of the potential outcomes that surround a person, a collective, or a situation, and access specific details regarding where they are now, what has led them there, and the trajectory they are on.

As creative consciousnesses, every action, every reaction, every decision, and even every shift of energy can entirely shift the reality we find ourselves in. It's a world that is so incredibly fluid and responsive to each one of us that no single outcome can ever be set in stone.

When it comes to collective timelines such as global events or Earth cycles, these are more stable, however. That's because the energy behind them comes from the power of many people, making them less likely to shift quickly. But on an individual level, timelines are highly malleable.

The skill that psychics have uncovered is the ability to perceive the timeline that an individual or a collective is currently most aligned with. Within that timeline, a psychic is able to perceive specific marker points and stepping stones that could correlate with particular times, dates, or even occurrences. This is the foundation of our predictions and how we're able to tell someone about something specific prior to it happening.

There's a great responsibility in delivering a psychic prediction, because when someone believes that what they've been told is guaranteed – as many do when they see a talented psychic – they begin to increase the likelihood of it becoming their reality through the power of belief and expectation. Even if it's not the reality they truly desire.

Many psychics are still operating from the outdated belief that they are fortune-tellers and that what they see is what will happen. But the more evolved and ethically grounded approach is to understand that our work is meant to empower someone's future, not dictate it.

Whereas in the past, psychic readings often left a person feeling powerless, subject to the will of fate, evolved psychic readings have the potential to offer a person broader insight into what they need to change or shift in order to align with the reality they actually wish to experience.

Because a psychic has the potential to perceive not only the trajectory a person currently finds themselves on, but also the alternate realities that are within their field of potential – the other versions of themselves they're entangled with – they can perceive exactly what needs to be done in order for the person to fully align with and achieve what it is they desire.

Psychics have the power to assist people in shifting timelines.

A reading I once did clearly demonstrated the creative power that each individual holds. It was for a woman in her forties who was desperate to be a mother. She had never been able to conceive and was in her sixth round of IVF, with her seventh and eighth already booked. The process was understandably painstaking and heartbreaking for her.

When I first connected to her energy, I could feel the undeniable longing she had for a child. Sadly, I also felt that children weren't coming to her in the direction she was heading.

But I knew that this wasn't about delivering bad news, it was about helping her to change her trajectory and shift the outcome. So I changed my focus to: *How can I help her align with the version of herself that does become a mother?*

That's when I sensed a deep wound – an unresolved pain related to her own mother. She confirmed it was something she had never faced. So it became clear to me that her fertility issues weren't only physical. They were energetic too, rooted in an emotional wound that had never been addressed.

I told her that this was what I felt was blocking her ability to conceive and that she needed to find a therapist, a healer, a facilitator of some kind to assist her in facing this emotional blockage. A colleague of mine came to mind, so I passed on the recommendation. I told the woman that I felt that if she was able to face and release this pain regarding her mother, she would be pregnant in October. I even relayed that I saw it happening naturally, without the need for IVF.

She followed through on my recommendation. She faced her blockage. And she naturally fell pregnant in October that year and became a mother.

The power to achieve her desired outcome was within the action that was required to align herself with it.

This is the key to aligning with your manifestations. And you don't actually need a psychic to tell you what you need to do, because your intuition is already telling you. It always does. You just need to listen and act.

There is an infinite number of timelines available to you, and not a single one is rigid in nature. Your free will is the one thing that can never be taken away from you as a spark of Source consciousness.

So, what's the difference between manifesting something and predicting it psychically? Truthfully, there is none. Both are rooted in the same principle, of perceiving potential timelines.

Predictive Insights

Psychic abilities often show up without us being aware of them. Many people receive predictive insights without even realizing – until after the event has occurred.

Here are some signs that your psychic abilities are already actively working within you:

+ You think of someone just before they call or text you.
+ You have synchronized thoughts with people you're close to (entangled with).
+ You think of someone you haven't seen in years and then bump into them soon after.
+ You think about how you need to buy a new umbrella and later that day find yourself caught in an unexpected downpour, thinking, *Damn – what are the chances of that?*

Your 'Spidey senses' are always communicating, whether you notice them or not. And they don't just nudge you about small things. They also reveal potential paths and outcomes, as well as bigger dreams and longings.

When you feel pulled toward a beautiful vision or idea, like a dream holiday, a new home, or a relationship, that's your higher self showing you what's possible. With enhanced intuitive awareness, the steps to align with that timeline will start revealing themselves too. And through acting upon them, you'll soon find yourself there, experiencing it for real.

As psychic beings, we can also connect to potential outcomes that are completely undesirable. We imagine worst-case scenarios and all the things that could go wrong. Sometimes they're just expressions of anxiety and sometimes they're genuine perceptions.

But here's the key: you get to choose which ones you align yourself with.

You do that by what you choose to invest in – by the state you choose to become.

The thoughts you give power to, align yourself with, and base your actions upon are how you navigate through potential timelines. They're determined by your lens of perception and are how you attune to the frequency of certain outcomes.

This is why worrying is like praying for the worst possible outcome. It's the fastest way to align yourself with the reality you're most dreading. It's one of the most important habits to break for anyone who's ready to experience a life of true expansive magic.

> The thoughts create the beliefs.
> The beliefs create the actions.
> And the combination of those creates
> the energetic alignments.

The more conscious you become of the timelines you're tuning into, the more intentional you can be about which ones you bring to life through your alignment.

Grounded Action

One of the most common missing links in manifestation is the grounded action that is required to actualize it.

When you're pouring every part of your energy and intention into manifesting something – something expansive and exciting – you may have a repeating thought about something you *should* do. It's usually the very thing you don't want to do. And it's the very thing that's keeping you from being a vibrational match with what you want to manifest.

It's only through actioning that step, through doing the thing you don't want to do, that your dream will move from the realm of potential into the realm of experience. That's how you break out of the paradigm you're currently operating within and expand into the one where your desire is already waiting. Just like my client who resisted facing the emotional blockage with her mother. She avoided it for years. But the moment she finally leaned in, she aligned perfectly with her deepest hope of becoming a parent.

The same applies in smaller, everyday ways. Say you're trying to manifest more clients. You're visualizing, calling them in, but something keeps nudging you to show up more consistently on social media. You resist. You hate the idea of being visible online. That's your intuition's way of telling you exactly what to do to manifest those clients.

Sometimes the pathway to a manifestation arrives as a simple, almost playful idea. That's exactly what happened when I manifested getting up on stage and meeting Kylie Minogue. The pathway? Buy a piece of paper and write her a message. That tiny action unfolded into perfection when the cameraman panned to me and Kylie turned her head at the exact moment my message was shown on the big screen.

I've had a few Kylie manifestations like this. Once, I found myself on her personal guestlist, with free VIP tickets to a sold-out show I couldn't get into, just hours before it began. Another time, I somehow ended up sitting in a small room with her and a world-famous choreographer while they gave advice to a group of dancers.

That one did involve telling a security guard that I was a dancer... which is technically true, if you count the sort of dancing that happens at 1 a.m. in a nightclub or bopping around the house while vacuuming. Somehow, he took me for the professional kind, and before I knew it, I was sitting in a room with Kylie and an A-list choreographer. Was it bold? Maybe. A little over the line into 'crazed superfan' territory? Probably. But hey, my intuition had told me exactly what to do, and it worked!

Both manifestations came to life through actioning an idea that dropped into my awareness while picturing myself there and trusting that it could happen.

And this is the whole point: You can use this inner guidance for anything your heart desires, whether it's playful, like my Kylie escapades, or a life-changing milestone. When you stop expecting the universe to simply drop things into your lap and instead act on the steps your intuition highlights, you manifest with remarkable precision and power.

Intuition is your soul's compass. It gives you instructions, and when it becomes a prioritized voice in your manifestation process, everything flows. Revelations, insights, and clarity begin dropping in. You'll know exactly what to do, and how to do it.

But there is no bypassing. No skipping the steps. No energetic shortcut. Every manifestation needs to be supported with the action that allows it in.

It takes equal parts belief, action, and energy to manifest a desired outcome.

Doubt must be replaced with conviction. Hesitation must be replaced with aligned action. And complacency must be replaced with energetic attunement.

You don't need to wait for a sign that something is 'meant to be.' You don't need to live under the belief that every part of your life has already been decided. While your soul's contracts may play a role in how you navigate reality, there are always multiple paths to fulfilling them. So, start taking those steps.

You are a powerful creator, not a passive participant.

> **Know this: You've only thought of something because it is within your realm of potential.**

I've heard people say, 'God wouldn't have put a dream in your heart if there wasn't a plan for it.' And there's deep truth in that. But what's often missed is that God isn't responsible for delivering the dream. You are. Because you are a piece of that Source.

> *'When you are in alignment with the soul, miracles become natural.'*
>
> Dr. Wayne Dyer

You're not a passive recipient of a definite fate, you're a powerful cocreator with the universe. So choose wisely about what to invest yourself in.

How much soul you bring to your manifestations will determine how soul-fulfilling those manifestations become.

Becoming Magnetic

To understand manifestation on a deeper level, we need to explore how energy moves through your quantum field and shapes your experience of reality.

Your energy field surrounds your body in a shape similar to an apple. Imagine the stem of the apple as your pineal gland, containing the tiny crystals that act as transmitters and receivers of frequency. Energy is processed here. It then moves through the body and is felt by the heart, where it gains an emotional charge. That emotional resonance continues through the rest of the body, creating a biological reaction, then flows toward the base of the spine and feet before looping outward around the field (like the skin of the apple), re-entering at the crown of the head.

This cyclical motion is constantly broadcasting and attracting energy. So, you're always manifesting your reality – through your thoughts, beliefs, feelings, and subconscious wiring. Intentional manifestation happens through aligning all this energy with what you want. Through becoming magnetic.

Feelings Are Key

At the core of every desired manifestation is one simple thing: a feeling.

Feelings are always the biggest drivers of our actions. Everything we do, we do out of a desire to feel a certain way. It's never truly about the money, the relationship, the recognition, or the lifestyle. What we long for is the *emotional experience* those things seem to promise – freedom, love, peace, excitement, confidence, security, joy, relief. Every manifestation is driven by a desire to feel differently.

And that's the key. Because if it's a feeling you're truly after, then the fastest way to align with a manifestation is to generate that feeling now, before anything has arrived.

This is what collapses time. This is how you become the version of yourself who already has what you want.

This is also where most people go wrong. They feel lonely, so they try to manifest a partner, for example. They visualize one, they 'put it out there' to the universe, but they continue to dwell in the predominant vibration of loneliness. And the universe doesn't respond to the vision, it responds to the feeling. That's what's rippling through their field, so that's what they attract more of.

Likewise, the key to manifesting financial abundance isn't imagining what you'll buy when it arrives. It's tuning into the feeling of abundance now, letting that feeling become the lens through which you perceive the world and experience yourself.

This is why people who are slightly delusional are often powerful manifestors. The 'De-lu-lu Manifestor' is someone who doesn't allow their external reality to dictate the vibration they're holding. They ignore the evidence around them, believe what they choose to believe, and stay within that frequency. While polarizing, it works.

A thought alone holds little power, but when it evokes an emotion, it becomes vibrationally potent. That emotion imprints the body and field, and you shift into the version of yourself who is already living that experience. The energy moves outward, entangling with vibrations of a similar resonance and drawing in experiences, people, and opportunities that align with it.

So, when you can feel the state you're seeking ahead of the evidence that it's coming, you don't need to chase it. You become it. And it's magnetized to you.

> **When you feel it, you radiate it.**
> **When you radiate it, you attract it.**

This is why your perception is everything. The way you see the world determines what you emotionally respond to, and therefore what you attract.

This is why people with a generally positive outlook tend to move through life with more ease and grace – what others call luck. If you've ever felt chronically unlucky, it might be time to examine your perspective.

Shifting your lens to one of optimism and gratitude raises your emotional resonance and your vibrational state of being. Gratitude in particular is a superpower, because when you feel grateful for what you've yet to receive, your field sends the message: 'I already have it.' You vibrationally entangle yourself with the version of yourself who lives that reality. It creates a feedback loop that says, 'I am already there.' And from that place, you can't help but become a match.

✦ ✦ ✦

Since your field of creation is always active, real change doesn't come from one-off visualizations or temporary excitement. Lasting manifestation is the result of consistent emotional and energetic discipline. The real work is in rewiring beliefs, shifting perspectives, and anchoring new emotional states over time.

But let's not forget, your soul's power is miraculous – and yes, you can absolutely use it to manifest miraculously. So let's practice that now.

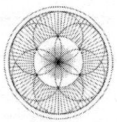

BECOMING THE VERSION OF YOURSELF WHO ALREADY LIVES YOUR DESIRED REALITY

This practice helps you step beyond visualization into vibrational embodiment — where soul energy, emotional resonance, and conscious intention merge to collapse time between you and your desired outcome.

You've already learned that all versions of yourself exist within the quantum field. That your desires come from your soul. That your feelings are key. This practice will help you attune to a version of yourself who already lives your desired manifestation and to claim their frequency now.

Use this for any specific desire you feel called to manifest. Return to it as many times as needed. Your ego may resist. That's natural. Keep choosing the higher frequency anyway.

1. Breathe deeply. Visualize your energy expanding outward from your center. Call on your soul's intelligence to take the lead.

2. Hold the desire in your heart. Remember, your soul led you to this desire for a reason. In this expanded state, set the intention to connect with the version of yourself who is already experiencing it. Trust that their energy exists in the quantum field. Tune into them.

3. Feel their essence. What does their energy feel like? What is life like for them with this desire fulfilled? What emotional states are they radiating? Gratitude? Confidence? Joy? What's changed for them?

4. As you feel into this version of yourself, you begin to entangle with their frequency. Allow your body to respond – let the feeling ripple throughout your entire being. Visualize every cell in your body and strand of DNA being imprinted with their frequency. Let your posture shift. Let your expression change. Let your breath deepen. You are becoming them now.

5. Feel it fully. Anchor it. Let their joy become your joy. Let their knowing become your knowing. Trust that this state is collapsing the time and space between you and the manifestation.

6. Move forward from this state. Let it inform how you speak, how you move through the world, how you show up. If your ego kicks in with doubt or limitation, gently return to the vibration.

Do this practice again if needed. It may take repetition. It may take time. But the more often you hold this frequency, the more you draw the manifestation into form.

You already know you are always manifesting. But now you're manifesting with soul power.

And here's what may surprise you: The power that magnetizes your desires is the very power that opens portals, defies the laws of physics, and allows you to commune with the unseen.

You've been using it all along.

Now it's time to understand how it really works.

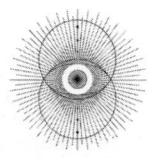

Chapter 14

MEDIUMSHIP: COMMUNICATING WITH THE SPIRIT WORLD

Now that you know that your connection to Spirit is your birthright, along with the energy that you need to harness in order to connect, let's explore how that connection actually happens. We'll begin by understanding the universal mechanics of mediumship, then dive into two distinct forms of communication: connecting with unfamiliar souls (evidential mediumship), and communing with your own loved ones in spirit.

The Mechanics of Spirit Communication

Spirit communication is the act of expanding your own field of consciousness, your own bubble of energy, and inviting another field of consciousness to step into that bubble. Then you attune to what subtly shifts within your field and begin interpreting it through the thoughts in your mind and the sensations in your body.

For communication with the spirit world to occur, there's always a vibrational gap that needs to be bridged. A kind of energetic portal that must be opened. And more often than not, this process happens unintentionally.

For example, in the time directly after a person passes, their energy is often felt with intensity. They appear in dreams, send signs, and make their presence known. That's because, in those moments, the doorway between worlds is wide open – held open by the sheer power of collective will.

So many people are thinking of that person, holding them in their hearts, mourning them, longing for closeness. That emotional energy pulls their spirit closer, making communication easier and more tangible. Their spirit isn't more powerful in that time, there is simply more power being offered to it by others.

But as time goes on and others shift their focus, that field of attention starts to thin. The doorway doesn't close, it simply becomes more subtle. That soul hasn't gone anywhere. But now they need to be invited in, this time through an intentional energetic process, one that mediums learn to work with consciously. The techniques vary, but the process is always the same.

There are three foundational steps. Whether you're connecting with loved ones, guides, or unfamiliar spiritual beings, this is the energetic structure that holds the work:

Initiate. Affirm. Surrender.

This is how an incarnate soul speaks to a discarnate one.

Initiate

You're the one who has a foot in each world, so you're the one who can initiate the connection. You're the one who consciously opens the door. Spirit may be sending signs and synchronicities, but to hold a sustained connection, you must create the energetic conditions for it.

That means:

+ Raising your vibration through intention and elevated emotion.
+ Evoking your soul power and expanding your field.
+ Getting still, receptive, and coherent with your intention.

This may require courage. But you never have to worry whether a spirit will actually show up. They will. Spirits are always eager to connect. They take every opportunity they can get to come forward and remind their loved ones of their ongoing presence.

Affirm

So, the moment you call Spirit in, something will happen – something subtle, something internal. It might be a sensation, a shift in thought, a wave of emotion, an image, a memory, a change in the space around you.

Whatever arises, you have to trust it. Even if it feels like nothing. Even if it's just a whisper. When Spirit connection is genuine, it doesn't usually feel grand or overwhelmingly supernatural. In fact, it often feels remarkably ordinary. Not because it's unimpressive, but because your soul recognizes the energy as familiar. So familiar, in fact, that you might even doubt it's there.

But if you want to commune with the spirit world, you must get quiet enough to feel the quiet things. Present enough to recognize when there's a spirit in your space.

What does it feel like when a spirit steps into your bubble, ready to connect with you?

You know that feeling you get when you're standing in line for something and you just know someone is standing unnecessarily close to you, encroaching on your space? I know you've felt it. Well, spirit communication is a similar feeling, albeit much nicer than that. It's the feeling of a presence within your own space, but one who's there with a pure, heartfelt intention. One who's eager and excited to connect with you.

The space around you becomes more tangible. Thicker, somehow. It begins to fill with an intelligent force, and it's always one that promises to demonstrate something profound whenever it's trusted to do so.

Spirits rarely come to connect with us from the space directly in front of us. They usually come from the side, or from behind. They join us from the space around us.

The moment you affirm what you're feeling – by acknowledging it rather than doubting it – you begin the flow of energy. Then you must be willing to allow your body, senses, and awareness to become the vessel through which the communication flows. You must surrender to the experience.

Surrender

Once the connection has been made, the communication must unfold naturally. The key is not to try to force or control it, but to flow with it. Allow it to lead you, not the other way around.

Don't grip. Don't analyze. Don't reach for proof. Just be fully present. Let the sensations deepen. Let the story unfold. Let the energy take you where it wants to go. And stay with it until the information becomes clear.

Communicating with Unfamiliar Souls

Mental mediumship, also known as evidential mediumship – where mediums communicate with unfamiliar souls, people they don't know – is the most widely recognized form of spirit communication. It's the type often demonstrated by mediums in personal readings or on stage in front of a live audience.

Mediumship has always required one thing above all else: proof. Before someone can truly believe that a medium is connected to their loved one in spirit, there must be *evidence* of it.

Although they have ascended back into something that is much greater than the person they were in their human lifetime, a spirit always presents themselves as the version of them that is most remembered. Because, if you went to a medium and they told you that an eternal spark of God consciousness with hundreds of different faces and expressions was coming forward to chat with you,

you wouldn't have a clue who they were talking about, would you?

That's why we begin by delivering facts, personal details, memories. These help identify the spirit and build trust in the person they're coming forward to connect with. They're how that person knows it's genuinely them there, communicating.

A whole world of information about their lifetime begins to become available. Their struggles, their flaws, their mistakes – all the things that are no longer a part of who they are, now that they're in their purest form – once again become available and recognizable within their field of energy.

I always say to my students, 'If someone was a piece of work in life, they're going to come through as a piece of work to me in a reading.' Meaning, even though a soul ascends into a grand spark of divine intelligence, presenting as their human self is the way they're going to be able to establish a meaningful connection.

But the purpose of evidence goes beyond validation; it also strengthens the energetic bond between the medium and the spirit. The more we understand the spirit's essence, the more their story unfolds.

Understanding Their Essence

A spirit's essence is the feeling of their soul in its purest expression: their love, personality, humor, passions, and what they were truly known and loved for beneath all the surface complexities of their human life. Through connecting to a spirit's essence, we gain an understanding of what it feels like to be connected to that person in a loving way.

By feeling into their essence, we begin to understand them.

Sometimes, even before we know who they are or what their relationship is to the person they've shown up for, we begin to feel who they truly are in a way that holds a deeper sense of resonance and meaning. That understanding is the real foundation of any successful connection.

A Stream of Communication

As a medium opens to their energy and connects to a spirit's energy, a merging begins. The energies start to overlap and entangle with one another. This creates a telepathic stream of communication.

At this point, we begin to notice thoughts, emotions, and memories that feel both familiar and foreign at the same time – like they belong to us, but also... not quite. We receive glimpses of stories, emotions, and experiences from the spirit's life that stand apart from our own inner workings.

In the beginning, only fragments may come through clearly, but with time, it's less like having a conversation *with* a spirit and more like *becoming* them for a moment. Their thoughts and memories feel as though they are ours, their perspectives, their feelings – even the way they speak or hold themselves – can influence our own body language and expression.

Through trusting and surrendering to all of those things, we move into our flow state and the magic of mediumship occurs.

Each detail builds a more vivid understanding of the communicator. As we connect more strongly with their essence, we develop a bond with them. The more we bond, the stronger the connection. We feel their presence within us. We feel their love for the person they've come to speak with being stirred within ourselves.

We might be reminded of our own life experiences when there's a match or a similarity, and we must learn how to separate what's ours from what's being shown to us.

With the right approach, the energy builds and rises. The information becomes clearer. When it flows, it feels effortless. The best evidence often arrives when we're least expecting it – when we're not forcing it, but allowing it. In that state, we become a great expression of our spiritual power and the relevant thoughts and impressions bubble up into our minds effortlessly as a result. We don't have to think about what's happening, we just flow.

In fact, there's a kind of synergy that takes over when you're strong in your power during a mediumship connection. It moves through you like a wave of momentum – before one piece of information finishes, the next one rushes in. You don't have to try. In fact, you can't stop it. It's like taking a few fast steps down a hill – suddenly, you're running!

Giving the Message

Eventually, we reach the most important part of any spirit communication: the message. What do they want to say? Why have they come?

Often, the message is simply one of love and presence. That brief moment of reconnection can mean everything. Other times, it's guidance, insight, or wisdom that the spirit wishes to offer.

Spirit communication is an art of interpretation. It's like playing a game of charades in your mind – decoding impressions, perceiving puzzle pieces and allowing them to come together and tell a full story. The spirit world often uses symbols and metaphors to share what they wish to share.

The more clearly we sense how a spirit's energy is experienced, the more easily we can access and understand the types of things they will wish their loved ones to hear – and deliver them from a place of understanding.

When we're deeply blended with them, we feel the sentiment of their message in our own awareness. Their love fills us as if it's our own. It's one of the most beautiful parts of this work – getting to feel the love of many people over and over again.

Validation

Working with unfamiliar souls requires practice, experimentation, and, most importantly, validation. You can only develop confidence in your connection when someone is present to confirm what's accurate and what isn't, and you have space to explore that.

It's how a medium can begin to understand their ability and learn to recognize how spirit communication presents when it's correct and how to identify when the mind is interfering. And yes, the mind does interfere. The monkey mind loves to jump in with doubt, stories, distractions, and noise. It often kicks in when your energy drops or when your trust wavers. This is why evidential mediumship is, in many ways, a balancing act between openness and discernment.

It all comes back to being attuned to what's happening within your awareness when you connect.

Communicating with Your Own Loved Ones

It often surprises people to hear that, for me as a medium, it's easier to communicate with other people's loved ones than it is to communicate with my own. The reason for this is sometimes the closer we were to someone in life, the harder it can be to feel them in Spirit – not because they aren't there, but because their energy has become a normal part of our inner world. And that familiarity can sometimes just feel like silence.

With all kinds of mediumship, when opening yourself to a connection, you're becoming aware of what subtle shifts are occurring within your own field of energy as you attempt to sense who has gathered with you. However, your loved ones in the spirit world are with you so often that when you shift your attention to find something different or unusual, there is often no foreign feeling within you at all. You have connected to an essence that is with you all the time – there is nothing out of the ordinary about that. So it can become difficult to recognize your loved one's presence.

Also, by already knowing their story, their energy, and who they have been, you don't have the opportunity to gather that information from them and build a trusted, validated connection in doing so.

The process, however, is still the same.

Initiate

First, as always, you create the energetic environment to connect by cultivating a heightened emotional state and evoking your power. Then, you set the intention to call the spirits forward to connect.

Affirm

Where, in cases of unfamiliar souls, you connect with them by getting a feel for their essence and how they are at the core of their energy, you connect with your own loved ones through imagining and remembering them. Instead of trying to discover how their essence feels, you remember what it feels like to be around them. You remember their presence, their humor, the way their love feels. You remember the sound of their voice and their laughter. You remember all the beautiful things about them, and while trying your best to not let it trigger or upset you and drop your power, you allow their energy to manifest within your space. You feel all of that energy, all of that love, as though it's right there next to you.

In acknowledging the feeling that occurs when you do so, you validate the connection, allowing it to strengthen.

Surrender

You're then in a space where your thoughts, senses, and emotions are being influenced by the spirit you're connecting with. Their sentiments will flood into you, you'll feel their love, you'll sense their messages, and you'll experience that connection as though it's another layer of yourself.

Your monkey mind will probably still be present, but you'll have a deep resonance from many of your thoughts and feelings, along with an inner knowing that they're from your loved one.

Validation

No matter how deeply you've felt it, how real that interaction has been, there will still usually be the human need to find validation and confirmation of the experience. Your ego is bound to look for flaws, find doubts, and question its legitimacy.

Except in rare circumstances, the information we receive from our own loved ones tends to be things that we already know. Their messages may be things that we could've assumed they would say, and simply have made up... But there are ways to receive undeniably clear validation of what our experience with them has been.

Spirits communicate through synchronicity. They show us signs, lead us to places, moments, and circumstances where we will be reminded of them. But these, too, can often be questioned and classified as 'coincidence.'

So, in order to receive validation from our own loved ones, we need to set up specific codes with them. This is what creates the opportunity for them to bring unquestionable signs into our world as confirmations of their presence.

Ask for a Sign

In the activated state, where a stream of communication is occurring, we can ask our loved one to show us something that will be used as confirmation of our shared experience. Then, when it comes into our orbit, we'll be able to wholeheartedly know that what we experienced in our connection with them was completely genuine and not based upon our own wishful thinking.

When it comes to the signs or symbols you're offered in response to your request, it's imperative to trust the first thing that you get, and to be open and optimistic about how it may show up in the world around you. Try to remain fluid, rather than defined, in your expectations.

Even as a professional medium, this is something I do with my own loved ones. So, I can assure you that the moment a sign is delivered – one you know to look out for – is a moment of pure magic, and heart-filling confirmation of your ongoing connection with your loved one. Over time, it strengthens your trust in the communication you have with them until it evolves to only needing to be on a telepathic level.

✦ ✦ ✦

When I was first taught this technique, I was on a cruise ship taking a development course with one of my mentors, the amazing medium Lisa Williams. I connected to my grandfather and asked him to show me a sign. Instantly, the image flashed in my mind of a sailboat moving over the open ocean. My grandfather was an avid sailor and fisherman – he even built his own sailboat – so I figured that this would be a pretty easy sign for him to show me, considering I was on a large boat myself at the time.

I presumed that I should be looking to the horizon for a sailboat, and that would be my sign. However, I now realize I might have thought that I'd just pictured something I was likely to see, and discredited that experience, had it happened that way. Fortunately, the spirit world operates with far more intelligence than that.

Right after the class where this was given to me as my symbol to look out for, I decided to go up to the pool and enjoy some sunshine. As I exited the elevator and took some steps outside, I noticed the on-deck band happened to be performing by the pool.

They were singing 'Sailing' by Rod Stewart – my grandfather's favorite song, the one that had been played at his funeral.

It blew my mind – the sign had come more instantaneously, more profoundly, and more intelligently than I'd ever expected. It brought a tear to my eye and filled my heart with love, knowing my grandfather was the one orchestrating it all.

The next morning we docked in Vanuatu. I exited the ship in a swarm of people piling onto a small jetty pathway. Walking in line, we passed several vendors selling souvenirs and trinkets, but I found myself standing right in front of a performer sitting in the middle of the jetty with his guitar while the crowd shuffled along either side of him. Can you guess what song he was singing?

That's right – he, too, was singing 'Sailing' by Rod Stewart.

The power of this sign made me awaken to the magnitude of the intelligence that the spirit world is operating within. Among those crowds of pushy and eager holiday-goers, it could have been so easy for me to walk right by without even noticing a person was there singing at all. But I happened to be there, right in front of him, as though he was an obstacle placed directly in my way, at the very moment he happened to be singing my grandfather's song.

It's moments like these that remove any doubt that's left within you and turn you into an embodiment of the undeniable truth that your loved ones are still with you. And that embodiment is often what allows you to communicate with them from that point on, in the simplest and most trusted way: thought transference.

This validation method has also allowed me to help people receive direct validation from their loved ones after a mediumship session. One of my favorite stories of all comes to mind here.

One day when I was doing my readings gig out the back of a crystal shop in Melbourne, a lady came in off the street for a reading. She said she'd been walking up and down all day, trying to decide whether to come in or not. She made it clear that she didn't believe in psychics or mediums, so she didn't know why she was there anyway. Something within her was just telling her to come in and see what all the fuss was about.

This particular client was in a very bad place mentally. The pressures of her life were causing her deep inner turmoil, to the point where she felt completely suffocated and was questioning her will to live. I could sense it within her from the moment she came in.

The pressure was on. I was only 19 years old and had not yet been told by someone that they were a non-believer prior to a reading. And I now had a client who was in a dark place and clearly wanting me to 'prove it' to them.

Luckily, that pressure converted into power, and the reading began effortlessly.

'Your father is here. He hasn't been gone for long. He's saying the name "Paul" to me.' The blood drained from her face. She began to tremble. 'My father, Paul. Passed away last year,' she muttered.

She'd walked in and sat straight down for her reading. She hadn't given a phone number or any personal information other than her first name, so any of the usual skeptic's accusations, like a Facebook or Google search, were out of the question.

The session continued on very clearly, very accurately, and she was astounded – and I relieved. But her ego had such a dominant hold on her that she still questioned, 'How can I be absolutely sure that this hasn't been some kind of trick, or cold-reading tactic?'

Even though her father had given her specific and intimate details of his life, it wasn't quite enough. She needed to have a message delivered to her directly – no middle man – from her father in spirit.

I instructed her to close her eyes and feel her father's presence with us in the room.

'He is here with us, right now. Ask him to show you something in your mind. Tell me the first thing you see. Don't question it, don't overthink it, just tell me what your first thought is.'

'I just see his hands,' she replied doubtfully.

I told her that sometime in the next day or two, she would see something or come across something that reminded her directly of her father's hands. Although I didn't have any idea of how a sign of that kind could occur, I trusted that it would happen.

We had five minutes left, and I had the inspired thought of pulling some oracle cards to close out the session and leave her with some further clarity to move forward with. The deck of cards I decided to use was one I hadn't used in over a year. Interestingly, something had been keeping me from heading out the door that morning. I had paced back and forth with the feeling that I was forgetting something, but I wasn't. So, I just decided to shove those cards in my bag and go. I hadn't used them for any other client that day, and this lady was my last.

My hand intuitively reached over for them and I began shuffling. As I shuffled, something miraculous happened. As though pulled by an imaginary force, a single card came out from the middle of the deck. It appeared to float out, almost as though it was moving in slow motion, and then it turned itself over and landed perfectly in the center of the table, facing upward.

It was titled: 'A father's love.'

The image was the outline of a father holding his daughter's hand. And where the hands were was a golden frame highlighting them as the centerpiece of the artwork. I couldn't have imagined a clearer or more divinely orchestrated sign from Spirit. Needless to say, she was convinced.

Before leaving, she gave me one of the most gratitude-filled hugs I've ever received and thanked me for changing her life. I told her that it was all her father's doing. He'd orchestrated it all for us both, every step of the way, from making me feel that I couldn't leave home that day without that deck of cards to pushing her through the door. I'd just been the conduit of all the love that he wished to express, and man, did he display it with some remarkable intelligence.

> **This form of communication is profound, extraordinary, and direct – and everyone is capable of experiencing it.**

It's simply a matter of creating the energetic environment for it to occur.

✦ ✦ ✦

After experiences and encounters like this, when there's enough trust in how easily you're able to communicate with your loved ones in spirit, they will simply drop into your thoughts. You'll hear their comments in the form of a thought like *This is what they would say right now*, and you'll think of them and their perspective or humor in specific moments. You may dismiss it as just a thought, but you'll know on a deeper level that they have genuinely inspired that thought at that moment.

Over time, your bond will become innate, you won't need to try to connect, and they'll be able to weave their way into your everyday life without you needing to do much work at all – the trust will simply be enough. It can be built by intentionally and ritualistically creating space to commune with these spirits, and through being open to receiving profound confirmations through synchronicity.

Let's drop into an exercise where you can take yourself to the perfect place to meet with your loved ones, build this connection, and ask them for the signs that they'll be able to bring into your orbit to strengthen the new type of relationship you now have.

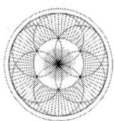

CONNECTING WITH YOUR LOVED ONES

Step 1: Be in a Quiet Space

- Choose a space where you won't be interrupted. Sit in a comfortable position, relax your body, and become present.

Step 2: Evoke Your Spiritual Power

- Turn your awareness to your energy and call your soul power to the surface. Allow your inner light to rise up and fill the space within you. Let it shine out around you, expanding softly and steadily. Have reverence for your light as your access point to Spirit.

Step 3: Expand Your Field and Shine Out as a Beacon

- With your light shining out, visualize your field growing larger. Expand your energetic space like a bubble opening outward. This creates the potential for your loved ones in spirit to step forward and meet you there.

Step 4: Feel a Loved One Come Close

- Bring to mind a loved one in the spirit world whom you'd like to communicate with. Feel them gathering next to you. Invite their presence. Picture them coming and sitting beside you.

Step 5: Remember Their Essence

- Start to feel into their essence. Remember what it feels like to be around them — their laugh, the sound of their voice, their charm, the way their love feels. Sense their humor, their mannerisms, their energy. Let those memories stir within you.

Step 6: Acknowledge Their Presence

- Notice how the atmosphere around you shifts. You might feel their hand on your shoulder. You might feel them beside you, behind you, or wrapping themselves around you. Let the love develop in this space. Let yourself sit with it without getting upset or triggered and losing the vibration you've built up.

Step 7: Allow Awarenesses to Arise

- Without asking questions or needing answers, stay in the love. In this space, you may become aware of something they want to share with you. There may be thoughts, memories, emotions, or insights. Just let what wants to rise come gently into your awareness. Don't force anything; remain in their presence and just see what comes.

Step 8: Ask for a Symbol of Communication

- Ask them to give you a symbol of your connection. Trust the first thing that drops into your awareness. Whether it's an image, a word, a memory, or a feeling, trust it without question. It will be something that later appears around you in the outside world as a confirmation of the experience.

Step 9: Thank Them and Close with Gratitude

- Thank your loved one for coming forward. Feel that gratitude. Gratitude from your heart helps anchor the connection in an ongoing way.

Step 10: Let the Symbol Confirm the Connection

- Carry the symbol with you and look out for it in the days that follow. It will find you. When it appears, let it be the confirmation that your loved one was truly communicating with you. Let it wash away any doubt and allow your heart to open even further to their continued presence and communication in your life.

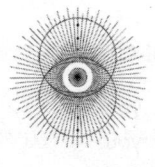

Chapter 15

RETURNING TO CONNECTION

An essential truth of the human experience is that at multiple points, each of us will walk through sadness, grief, pain, and despair. There is no path of awakening that bypasses life's heaviness. And true spiritual connection doesn't require us to avoid these places; it requires us to bring our soul into them.

So much of this book has been about elevated states – about joy, love, gratitude – and their power to connect us to the divine. This chapter is here for the moments when that feels impossible. When you're not in a high vibration. When your heart is broken or your energy is low. When you feel lost in the heaviness of this world.

Remaining Connected in Dark Times

Toxic positivity is the shadow aspect that sometimes comes out of the understanding that elevated states of emotion are what allow us to remain connected and powerful. This is the perspective that you can only be connected if you're on top of the world and vibing high. That idea not only creates shame around very natural human emotions, but it robs those emotions of the transformative power they hold.

When we're in the depths of a dark night of the soul – grieving, mourning, releasing – is when we feel the need for a connection with the divine more than ever.

We need a message. We need a sign. We need to feel the presence of our loved ones in spirit. Pain doesn't stop any of that happening. Our ego, on the other hand, can.

Pain is often the doorway through which more light is found.

It's in times of suffering that many people decide to attempt to make a connection to a higher power for the first time. The desperation that they're feeling is often a catalyst for even sworn atheists to find themselves praying.

Prayer that rises out of desperation is actually one of the purest acts of spiritual connection, because it comes from a full surrender. It's the ego laying down its armor and saying, 'I can't do this alone.' And more often than not, it's in these moments that people first feel something that truly helps them – a presence, a sense of peace, a return of hope. *They begin to remember.*

Some of the most life-changing spiritual moments happen in the very pit of darkness. Not because the darkness is a good place to be, but because it makes us reach for something more. Reach for connection. Reach for remembrance. And it is in that reaching that we awaken.

And the reason for this is that the cracks are where the light gets in.

Remember, you're always the only one who holds the power to pull yourself through. You have a team of helpers behind you – loved ones, guides, ancestors, a spiritual army who are ready to offer their hands. But they cannot reach you if you don't first reach for them... with the tiniest breath of hope.

That's all it takes.

Spirit responds to our willingness. It responds the moment we stop feeling sorry for ourselves and begin to genuinely seek a route out of our darkness.

Being Honest

This doesn't mean you have to fake positivity and attempt to bypass your emotions, though. In fact, quite the opposite.

Remaining connected during times of heaviness doesn't mean pretending you're okay or focusing on better things. It means allowing yourself to surrender into *every* emotion, while still honoring your inner light.

Let yourself cry out what needs to be cried out. Let yourself feel every bit of grief, fear, and loss.

You must allow yourself to feel it all. Rage. Cry. Mourn. You have to let the storm of feelings pass through you without letting your ego convince you that the storm *is* you.

Don't let your ego trap you there. You have to remember that it's just weather – and there is blue sky on the other side of it.

You don't need to fake being positive to be spiritually connected. You only need to remain willing, stay open, and then, when the time is right, rise again. And when you do, you rise stronger, wiser, and more connected than before.

If you can rediscover your light while you're in the dark, you'll be more powerful than ever, once you've made it out to the other side.

Enjoying the Glimmers

The higher intelligence within all of us knows that sometimes all it takes is a glimmer, a small flicker of hope, to completely alter our trajectory and pull us from a dark place.

Glimmers are those lovely little moments that light us up, even when everything else feels heavy. Allow yourself to receive them.

Even in grief or pain, let yourself feel the beauty of a song, enjoy the warmth of the sun, fully receive a kind message, or smile at a memory that comes to mind. That isn't bypassing. That's giving yourself grace and allowing yourself a moment to pull your head out of the darkness and breathe.

In times of loss, we must remember too that the grief is only ours. We aren't holding it for our loved one. They are in a beautiful place. They are still with us. They are eager for us to feel their presence again.

So, don't let your ego shame you for feeling joy, or letting a funny memory about that loved one make you giggle. Those are the very glimmers that are taking you to a place where you'll be more easily able to sense them again.

Coming Back to Your Natural Rhythms

Here's something we rarely stop to think about...

We weren't made to live in a world like this. We weren't designed to spend most of our waking hours inside buildings, glued to screens, hooked on stimulants, eating chemically processed food, or drinking water treated with chemicals and pumped through metal pipes.

We weren't meant to be bombarded with every global tragedy broadcast directly to our pocket or living room, or to feel the weight of the world on our chest before we've even had our morning coffee.

We weren't made for the pace, pressure, or pollution of this world, but we've been taught to accept them as normal.

Most of us are wired to experience life through stress. Rushing from one thing to the next. Wishing the days away just to have two short days of freedom. Living under constant financial, emotional, and societal pressure. Always trying to keep up. Always behind. Always just one step away from burnout.

Whether it's the news cycle, work obligations, or the sheer pace of modern life, stress has become our baseline. And when that stress builds, we often cope in ways that only deepen our disconnection – escapism, addiction, frustration, illness.

Eventually, the smallest things start to tip us over the edge. We snap at strangers in traffic. We get irritated by people walking too slowly. We hand over our peace (and power) to things we can't control, all while wondering why we feel so depleted.

Stress is the fastest way to kill our spiritual connection.

It keeps us scrambling, chasing, and jumping ahead of ourselves, which means it pulls us out of the present moment entirely. And our spirit can't remain where we won't.

It is only in presence, openness, and stillness that intuition arises. That soul guidance can reach us and Source move through us. Without those qualities, our energy stays scattered and unreachable, even to us.

So many of the things we overlook, such as our environment, our routines, our mindset, have the deepest effect on our spiritual connection. Why do we race home at the end of the day but forget to put our feet on the grass and just breathe? Why do we let a stranger's slowness ruin our mood? Does sitting at a red light for an extra minute really need to take us out of alignment and deplete us?

What if our exhaustion, our brain fog, our sadness, our chronic stress – what if all of it is simply our system responding to a world we were never designed for?

What if our symptoms are actually signals?

And what if fresh air, real food, clean water, rest, movement, and time in nature aren't just 'nice ideas' that we 'probably don't have time for,' but are necessary for our quality of life and spiritual connection?

Because... we *are* nature.

Yes, you're made of the same particles as the ocean and trees. Your body is in its most natural environment when it's at one with the Earth. That's why a walk under trees or time spent by natural running water immediately shifts your mood. That's why you expand your field of energy just by placing your feet on the soil.

That's your energy saying, 'Ahh, that's what was missing!'

When any living being is removed from its natural environment, it will suffer. Physically, emotionally, spiritually, the effects are inevitable.

Take orcas, for example. In the wild, they're majestic, intelligent, and free. They travel vast distances each day, dive deep into the ocean, and move constantly. But in captivity, they're confined to small tanks, unable to swim, roam, or live the way they're meant to.

Over time, their health deteriorates. Their fins collapse. Their behavior changes. They become lethargic, depressed, sometimes aggressive. Attacks on trainers become more common. Meanwhile, in the wild, orca attacks are nearly unheard of. And when they live as nature intended, orcas live much longer lives.

Why? Because when a being is cut off from what they were made for, they disconnect, and they suffer.

What's happening to these orcas is happening to the human race, on a grand scale.

The majority of the world's population now lives in concrete cities – far from nature, bombarded by artificial light, noise, chemicals, and a constant stream of information that was never meant to fit inside the human body or mind.

We're breathing in pollution, eating food with ingredients that look like a math equation, and scrolling through reminders of the darkest and harshest realities of this world before we've even left our bed. Then we wonder why we feel uninspired, disconnected, and unwell.

It's not you. It's your environment. But it *becomes* you when you stay in it.

That's why remaining connected to your soul in this world takes conscious effort. It takes discipline. It takes choice. You have to carve out space to return to yourself – because this world won't hand it to you.

Choosing Differently

Spiritual connection on a daily level begins with noticing how your priorities are making you feel and, if necessary, choosing differently. Why is this?

> **Your emotional state is your signal. How you feel, moment to moment, is your vibration.**

And that vibration is the foundation of your spiritual connection.

So, being a conscious human means recognizing what drains you and choosing differently. It means understanding what you need to thrive and giving it to yourself. Not just once – I mean getting your fix of relaxation and foot-to-earth connection as a scheduled part of your week.

There are so many factors pulling people away from their own divinity. The fast pace. The distraction. The pressure to do, to provide, to succeed. There *is* magic here. There is beauty, wonder, awe. But to see it, to feel it, you have to *choose* to look for it. You have to build the kind of life that allows it to reach you.

That doesn't necessarily mean moving to the mountains (unless that's what calls you). It means creating regular moments in your life when your nervous system can settle and where your energy can recalibrate.

That might look like:

- ✦ Prioritizing daily time outside in nature – even just a five-minute walk or grounding yourself on the grass or sand with the sunlight on your skin.
- ✦ Watching a sunrise or sunset once a week.
- ✦ Meditating each morning, even if only for a few rounds of conscious breathing.
- ✦ Starting your day with yoga, or by dancing in your lounge with headphones on to your favorite music!

Whatever it is that brings you back to your center, make time for it.

Joy, beauty, peace, and presence aren't luxuries – they're vital for your life-force energy.

And as much as this may seem obvious, it sure is easy to forget.

So, always remember that when you slow down, come home to your body, feel the earth beneath your feet, and breathe with intention, your energy responds, your frequency rises, your intuition sharpens, and your soul takes the wheel again.

And suddenly, the things that used to pull you under lose their grip.

You remember who you are and that you're not here to keep up with a world that has forgotten its own rhythm, you're here to create your own.

And *that* is power.

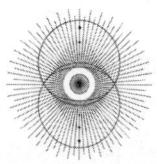

CONCLUSION: THE GUIDING LIGHT TO PURPOSE

So, now that you've accessed this power, what will you do? Where will it lead you? What greatness is awaiting you on the other side of clearing out the debris and stepping even further into the embodiment of your soul?

The best part is, you don't have to know that yet, because your soul already does.

You find yourself at one with the deepest sense of purpose through following your soul's nudges and simply living as a greater embodiment of it.

All the magic that's been awakened within you throughout this journey is only the beginning. By putting the insights, practices, and perspectives shared in this book into motion, you'll find that the pathway you're now on gets grander, more wondrous, and more expansive, the longer you stay on it.

The nature of spiritual evolution is to constantly be presented with the opportunity to advance. So, on that path, there are many doorways, many opportunities to go higher and higher.

Creating space for your soul self to rise within you means that you become intuitively led, able to be guided and directed by the intelligence of your higher self to the people, places, opportunities and experiences that will be enriching to your life.

Sometimes these nudges can be as simple as deciding to take the scenic route instead of the highway and seeing a beautiful rainbow as a result of doing so. It could be that you feel guided to make an effort to start a conversation with someone in the street and end up having a heartwarming interaction or even an ongoing connection with them. When you begin to act upon the subtle impressions and nudges, no matter how purposeless they may seem at the time, you're trusting the intelligent guiding force that is your higher self and you're rewiring yourself to act upon your intuition, which is your soul's intelligence.

Those simple little nudges that you decide to trust then become soul ignitions that lead you to wondrous and magical experiences, and even life-altering decisions, and toward a profoundly connected and fulfilling existence.

Keeping the Ego in Check

Your soul can show you the doorway, fill you with an intuitive flame of excitement, and tell you in the core of your being that something is right for you. But with every step you take toward growth, mastery, and expansion, you will be met by new patterns and behaviors of the ego mind that become the challenges associated with your ongoing growth. Each time you're about to level up and start operating within a new paradigm, you'll be presented with that 'thing' you don't want to do. As you begin to dream bigger and bigger, your fear of following the soul nudges will remain present. That never entirely goes away.

The best thing you can ever do is follow that internal compass by not allowing your ego to stop you in your tracks.

You can always count on it to make an attempt to do so, especially as you begin to explore uncharted territory, no matter how much you feel you have it under control. And your ego is guaranteed to be with you right up until your final breath – but you can evolve around it.

If you find yourself thinking that you have completely rid yourself of your ego, it probably has a bigger hold on you than ever before. Don't let it trick you. Stay aware. Keep it in check. And stay as aligned with your inner divinity as you can.

Embodying Your Soul

You are an emanation of God. A spark of creation. A conscious extension of the universe itself. The soul within you holds memory beyond time, wisdom beyond comprehension, and power beyond your wildest imagination.

And now, you've remembered.

Through these pages, you've explored the truth of incarnation, the nature of the spirit world, the mechanics of manifestation, the communication between dimensions, and the miraculous abilities that arise when the soul is embodied.

These teachings aren't meant to be understood. They're meant to be lived. So, keep deepening your bond with your soul. Seek out enriching ventures. Initiate mystical experiences.

Connect with the spirit world and allow the love and guidance of those who are there to be present in your life.

Access your divine creative power to become magnetic to experiences, opportunities, and encounters that increase the value of your existence.

Cultivate enough soul embodiment, and things you never thought possible will become your lived experience.

You have opened a doorway to the miraculous. The abilities that are emerging within you now are ones that will transform your existence from this day forward. Maintain your practice. Keep this enchanting moment going. Move deeper and deeper into the untapped realms of your own potential.

Let this be a beginning. Not of more seeking, but of deeper embodiment.

You already know enough. You already *are* enough. What matters now is how willing you are to allow your soul to lead you further into greatness.

From this point onward, your practice is surrender and expansion. Your power is in your alignment.

The more you trust the intelligence of your soul, the more your life will reflect that power back to you. The more you honor your inner knowing, the more clarity, synchronicity, and miracles will surround you.

Live with as much joy, as much playfulness, and as much optimism as you possibly can. This world wasn't designed to be taken that seriously. It isn't the be-all and end-all of your existence, it's a glimmer in the eternity of your existence.

Let this be your truth now...

You aren't becoming a powerful spiritual being, you are already one.

Now embody it.

Live as it.

Speak as it.

Walk as it.

Create as it.

And let the world feel your light. Don't hold back any of that magic that your soul came here to share.

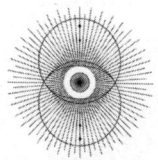

CLOSING INVOCATION

P lace your hands on your heart, take a deep breath, and repeat the words below:

Divine light that I am,

I evoke your presence,

I surrender to your intelligence,

I move by your guidance.

I have reverence for the infinitely grand light that I am,

and even greater reverence for the light that I was born out of.

I honor the journey I am on.

I remember that it is temporary.

*I let joy, wonder, reverence, and love lead
me through every step of the way.*

I remain embodied as the divine force that I am.

I integrate my light through all of my layers.

I feel its glow from within me,

its power as it enriches me,

and its unconditional love as it ripples through me.

This is who I am.

This is what I am.

This is the only part of me that will always remain true.

I am the light of creation.

*I promise myself to live with remembrance
of this truth from this day onward.*

I remember who I am.

And so it is.

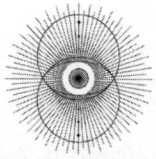

FINAL NOTE

Thank you for being on this journey with me. This book is more than pages and words, it is a transmission. A gift from my soul to yours. An activation. A remembering. And your arrival here, at the very end, tells me that something deep within you has already begun to awaken.

Maybe you read this to reconnect with a loved one in spirit. Maybe you were searching for answers, healing, guidance, or something you couldn't even name. But whatever led you here, I know you didn't come by accident.

You and I are more connected than you may think.

Your soul is and always has been leading you. And now you're following.

And the most exciting part? This is only the beginning.

I hope this book has reminded you that you're never alone. That you're more powerful than you've been taught. And that your soul isn't just watching your life unfold, it's creating it.

The journey ahead is a magical one. Trust that.

From the depths of my soul, thank you for letting me be a part of your remembering.

It's been my honor to guide you, I am proud of you, and I write this message with a heart full of gratitude for you.

With love,

from your friend,

Sean Collyns

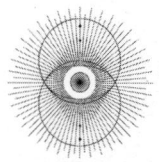

FURTHER READING

If you'd like to explore in more detail any of the topics covered in this book, I would recommend taking a look at any of the below titles.

Becoming Supernatural: How Common People Are Doing the Uncommon, by Dr. Joe Dispenza (Hay House, 2017)

Dying to Be Me: My Journey from Cancer to Near Death, to True Healing, by Anita Moorjani (Hay House, 2012)

Embracing Eternity: the Amazing Truth About Life After Death That Will Change Your World, by Tony Stockwell (Hodder & Stoughton, 2007)

Journey of Souls: Case Studies of Life Between Lives, by Michael Newton (Llewellyn Publications, 2010)

Many Lives Many Masters: The True Story of a Prominent Psychiatrist, His Young Patient and the Past-life Therapy That Changed Both Their Lives, by Dr. Brian Weiss (Piatkus, 1994)

The Power of Now: a Guide to Spiritual Enlightenment, by Eckharte Tolle (Yellow Kite, 2001)

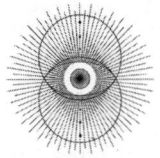

ACKNOWLEDGMENTS

There are many who played a part in bringing this book into creation. My first acknowledgement goes to Spirit, who I am forever grateful to be an ambassador for. Without their willingness to work with me in this way, there would be no book in the first place.

This project began in the most divine way. Writing a book was nothing but a distant dream, with no immediate plans to pursue it. Then, in a conversation, I mentioned Hay House as a dream partnership for 'one day.' The very next morning, an email arrived from a Hay House editorial director. No prior connection – just perfect timing, and a sign from Spirit that the time was already here.

Which leads me to the incredible team at Hay House, who have been nothing short of extraordinary in helping me bring this to life. To Helen, who was my first doorway into this wonderful company. To Michelle, whose expertise and power shine through, bringing me so much confidence. Special thanks to Kezia, Grace, Cathy, and the rest of the team who assisted me along the way. And a big thank you

Acknowledgments

to Lizzie, my editor, who brought clarity and flow into my words in a way that was truly masterful.

Thank you to Anita Moorjani, for writing my foreword – your words moved me deeply and opened this book with such beautiful energy, just like yours.

To my parents, Emma and Peter, thank you for always supporting me 100 percent on the pathway I've been called to in this life. Not once did you ever try to steer me away from what I was meant to do in this world. Thank you for your love and support, in a myriad of ways.

To my sister Briarly for walking this journey of exploration and expansion with me from the very beginning. For being there through so many of my firsts and sharing the excitement with me – without a doubt, we've done it many times together before. And for your contribution to this project, by encapsulating the essence of this book in your incredible artwork, and for being a place of reflection and support throughout the writing process.

To my dear friend Milly, thank you for celebrating the wins, for your heartfelt love and support, and for always lifting my spirits when the workload felt heavy. Yours is the kind of friendship that's hard to find.

To my Grandmothers, Mona and Judy – thank you for your unconditional love, and for always expressing your pride in me.

Then to my mentors: Debbie, my 'Spirit Momma,' the first to awaken this potential within me. To Tony and Lynn, who've given me as much wisdom and knowledge as they have laughter and love. To Lisa, for recognising something in me and taking me under her wing. And to Dianne – our friendship may seem unlikely, but when souls are this familiar, nothing is unlikely. You have each shaped me in ways I can never repay.

Thank you to my clients, my students, and to you, the readers, for joining me in this magical venture. None of this would be possible without your support.

To all the friends and loved ones who cheered me on, thank you for the love.

And finally, last but certainly not least, thank you to my person, Sam. You keep my feet on the ground, my heart full of love, and my world together.

And to our fur babies, Presley and Pumpkin – thank you for your purrs and cuddles, and being the best writing assistants I could have asked for. Even though you distracted me and sat on my laptop constantly.

My love and deepest appreciation goes out to each of you.

ABOUT THE AUTHOR

Sean Collyns is an internationally renowned psychic medium, spiritual teacher, and author whose work has impacted thousands of people worldwide. Known for his remarkable accuracy and powerful abilities, he has earned global recognition, with sold-out courses and retreats, a celebrity clientèle, and a waitlist for readings that stretches into the thousands.

As a devout teacher of the spiritual arts, Sean leads extensive development programs and seminars, empowering individuals to strengthen their own spiritual connection. His teachings have helped many students become successful psychics and mediums, furthering his reputation as a respected mentor within the field.

Recognized as a leading voice in modern mediumship, Sean is celebrated not only for his evidential accuracy, but also for his ability to guide others in unlocking their own divine potential. His work illuminates the intelligence of the spirit world, the limitless possibilities of soul embodiment, and the miracles that unfold when we expand into our divine potential.

@seancollynsmedium

www.seanpsychicmedium.com

TRANSFORM YOUR DAY— ANYTIME, ANYWHERE

With the **Empower You** Unlimited Audio *App*

> ★★★★★ **Life changing.**
> My fav app on my entire phone, hands down! – Gigi

Unlimited access to the entire Hay House audio library!

You'll get:

- 600+ soul-stirring **audiobooks** to expand your mind
- 1,000+ **meditations** for restful sleep, morning focus, and gentle healing
- Bite-sized audios **under 20 minutes**—perfect for busy days
- **Exclusive talks** you won't find anywhere else
- **Daily affirmations**
- Fresh content added **every week** to fuel your journey

Listen to the audio version of this book!

> Driving, yard work, and housework have been **transformed**!
> – Ruffles27

Scan the QR code to start listening or visit **hayhouse.com/unlimited**

CONNECT WITH
HAY HOUSE
ONLINE

🌐 hayhouse.co.uk   **f** @hayhouse

📷 @hayhouseuk   🦋 @hayhouseuk.bsky.social

♪ @hayhouseuk   ▶ @HayHousePresents

Find out all about our latest books & card decks • Be the first to know about exclusive discounts • Interact with our authors in live broadcasts • Celebrate the cycle of the seasons with us • Watch free videos from your favourite authors • Connect with like-minded souls

'*The gateways to wisdom and knowledge are always open.*'

Louise Hay